Contents

Acknowledgements

Our grateful thanks are due to Jackie French, ably assisted by Lynda Purnell, for slaving away over a hot word-processor, and to Gillian Hatch, our 'local editor'. Thanks, too, to all colleagues, mentors, teachers, students, pupils and others who, one way or another, provided the raw material.

PART ONE

Introduction

> In my books I do like to make fictional use of the materials I assemble or put together, and I deliberately make fictional constructions with authentic elements.
>
> M. Foucault

The idea for this book came from involvement in a research project, the Mentoring in Schools project, funded by the Esmée Fairbairn Charitable Trust between September 1993 and July 1995. The national research project was a collaborative project between six universities, namely Keele, Leicester, the Manchester Metropolitan University (MMU), Oxford, Sussex and Swansea. Each university had a focus and worked jointly with schools and mentors. Locally the project in Manchester was similarly collaborative between five primary schools from surrounding LEAs and the project team from the Didsbury School of Education.

The book also draws on local evaluation studies of previous pilot projects such as the Articled Teacher Scheme and partnership initiatives with primary schools, undertaken with students, mentors, headteachers, and university tutors during the period 1993 to 1997.

From these projects a rich source of data has been gathered, which covers teachers as mentors; students as learners; tutors as supervisors; children, parents and governors as 'clients'. This data has been presented in story form. We have amalgamated characteristics of the schools, mentors, students, tutors and pupils in order to fictionalise the research data. In this way we hope to tell the stories of the 'stakeholders' (a term we used in the project before it became politically fashionable) and by developing the use of 'fictional critical writing', Winter (1988) and Rowlands (1990), to present case stories. Teacher biography and teachers' stories are well-developed methodologies, Ball and Goodson (1985), Thomas (1995), Walker (1981) and Dadds (1995), but the approach taken in this book differs from these in its fictional setting and fictional characters. It relates, we believe, also to the emerging 'professional knowledge landscapes' and the 'ideas of secret, sacred and cover stories' as written about by Clandinin and Connelly (1996) in their focus on teacher stories and school stories as new ways of relating to professional life in schools, which they hope will stimulate new research questions which are more pertinent to practitioners and schools.

This is, therefore, different from the 'book from the project'. It may well be unique in its design but if so, that is largely by accident. We set out with the intention of 'telling tales', adopting a sort of 'Canterbury Tales' approach to school-based teacher education. Hopefully, the time is right for what we have tried to create, namely, a readable, interactive book which presents the phenomenological aspects of school-based training, the human face of mentoring, and which tells how people actually experience school-based teacher education partnerships The book seeks to both entertain and inform. The characters are fictional, but they are also real, in that they are based on real data collected through interview, observation, questionnaire and through teachers' enquiry into their own practice and schools. All the teachers involved in the research project undertook their own lines of enquiry, as co-researchers in the project. The fictionalising of the data and of the setting, the Jemima Johnston Primary School, allows us to disguise cases and people, thereby protecting the confidentiality of sources.

A fuller discussion of the methodology and of the use of narrative and fiction in educational research is to be found in Part Three.

Each of the tales is followed by a section entitled 'Commentary and Matters for Discussion'. Our intention has been to pick out a number of issues which arise from the tales and highlight them in the hope that they will promote further discussion. Unsurprisingly, several issues recur. If we had tackled in any depth all the issues which could be generated from the early tales in the book we would have had left nothing for later and the reader might never have reached 'later'. Indeed within the wordage formula to which we have been working, there might never have been a 'later'. As a result, from any one tale we have been highly selective about the issues explored. By the end, however, we hope that what we see as central issues will have emerged as a result of treating topics in different ways. Some topics we have treated incrementally, returning to them again and again. Others we have given an 'in depth' treatment at the end of a particular tale. The term 'in depth' is relative. Since one of our intentions is to point to useful further reading, it would be silly to claim that we are dealing with something 'in depth' when what we are actually doing is directing the reader to what might be a large chunk of a whole book or to a journal article, containing substantial discussion well beyond the scope of this book.

The further reading and the references in each commentary are themselves selective, based upon the topics we have chosen to explore. We try to show the connections; at least, the connections we perceive. However a full bibliography is to be found at the end. Hopefully, the suggestions for further reading and the bibliography will be helpful to teachers and others writing about mentoring and school-based training as part of their work for advanced qualifications.

In summary, whilst we hope the book will be widely read, it is essentially a book to be used – by all those involved in any way in school-based training. The fictional tales have their roots in fact; the issues are the issues we choose to select from the tales; the reading is the reading we think makes for useful signposts if you go down our road. If, however, you find different issues or would identify other reading, or would even give the tales different endings, the book will still have served its purpose.

Beneath the stories lie:

- questions concerning the culture and ethos of primary schools which enhance or hinder staff and student development,
- the centrality of the question of the impact of school-based teacher education on pupils' learning, behaviour and attitudes,
- the inherent tensions in the roles of teachers and tutors who must both support and assess students in classrooms,
- the dilemmas faced by all participants, both professional and personal, as collaboration in the education of teachers raises issues of loyalty and confidentiality and causes teachers to examine their professional and ethical codes,
- practical 'nitty gritty' issues to do with the management of school-based teacher education in primary schools: structures, funding, strategies, practices and staff development,
- issues of student entitlement, moderation and quality assurance in collaborative work between university and schools; issues of student rights, the resolution of conflict and the provision of pastoral care, especially where these appear to clash with the rights of significant others,
- the perspectives of other 'clients', such as parents and governors who have an influence on the provision for school-based teacher education.

The perspective of each 'stakeholder' and the 'stake' of each was and remains different and distinctive. The interaction of the individuals produces both problems and opportunities alongside tensions which can prove either creative or destructive. Throughout the book we hope to uncover progressively the subtleties of the interactions which frequently offer ways forward. The book aims to speak directly to teachers, tutors and students about the problems encountered in school-based training. It, hopefully, suggests ways to resolve these, sometimes with a light-hearted approach, although always mindful of the need to stress professionalism. The book will, it is hoped, aid the further development of mentorship, management of school-based training and collaborative work between students, teachers and tutors.

No one featured in the fictional tales actually exists with the exception of Her

Majesty's Chief Inspector, Chris Woodhead and the Chief Executive of the Teacher Training Agency (TTA), Anthea Millet, who make the most fleeting of appearances in non-speaking parts. Individuals were allocated names randomly, although just occasionally we have attached the name of a highly respected colleague to a particularly unlovable character.

The story begins in the early days of primary partnerships, somewhere around early 1994, and the scene depicted in the second chapter, 'The meeting', chronologically the first of the events was, we think, fairly typical of what many schools and universities engaged in as they groped their way forward to implement Circular 14/93.

PART TWO

CHAPTER 1

Paula's story: struggle

The 'phone call which I had just answered from Derek Wilson, the head of the Jemima Johnston Primary School, asking me if I could make a Staff Development Day four weeks hence, had triggered off my memories of Paula and her placement there almost three years earlier . . .

The first inkling I had that one of my more thoughtful, caring, student-centred decisions had gone badly wrong came with the 'phone call from Tom. Tom is not my favourite mentor. It is not that he doesn't dedicate himself to the task of mentoring; he does, almost obsessively so, and he keeps copious notes. He also writes copious notes on the student files whenever he gets hold of them. Sometimes he gets hold of them by rummaging in their bags and cases when they are not there. It used not to matter whether they were there or not, until the year when one of our more assertive students bit his head off when he went into her Tesco bag. Indeed she barely stopped short of biting his hand off. Tom received a lecture on privacy and the invasion of space which should have contributed significantly to his personal and social education. In the event it made a small but significant dent in his rhinoceros skin. He still goes for files with the persistence of a sniffer dog but his solution to the problem as he sees it is not the more obvious one of asking for files, politely, at a convenient time; his solution is to avoid confrontation by waiting for an opportunity when there is no one to confront before digging up the bone. He will then write relentlessly, drawing upon his copious notes.

Some students have found him a good mentor – usually those with few ideas and a poor self-image. Such students he has tended to relieve of any responsibility to think about their teaching. He has handed them 'good ideas', lesson plans, and even worksheets, and then been lavish with his praise for their creative thinking, sound planning and good quality resources! Criticism has been common, however, about the pace, delivery and quality of relationships with the pupils. A few students have been happy with that; well attested by their parting gifts and Christmas cards. Tom is very proud of these souvenirs or trophies which he takes home to his wife. He has told me that he always discusses the students in detail with his wife. He worries sometimes about how well he is doing as a mentor, but draws comfort from her reassurance that he is extremely conscientious and very kind. I assume that he demonstrates similar qualities in his home life. His wife is a student teacher too, mature obviously, and not at our university. Sometimes I wonder about *her* file. Tom explained from the outset of his becoming a teacher-tutor and a mentor that it was his wife's experiences that had persuaded him to volunteer for the task. His headteacher, Derek, had been happy to take up the offer and make use of his very special insights. As I said, some students have appreciated his commitment. Most find him a pain, and say so to me, or to tutors who refer their complaints on to me. Either way I have become used to complaints about Tom: bag snatcher, invader of space, critic extraordinary, professional heavy breather and King of the Cloners.

This time, however, the phone call heralded a complaint, not about Tom, but from Tom. About me. Now Tom, along with his other qualities, is a direct descendant from Uriah Heap. His complaints about students, while carrying very clear messages about the shortcomings of our courses, our deficiencies of preparation, our poor quality students and our inadequate tutors, always come obsequiously packaged. The things under the stones may be undesirable. Oh, but the stones . . . so beautiful, so carefully arranged, so fine when polished. Usually much credit has been attributed to me, shining like a beacon, while under my good light I enable him to rectify the deficiencies he has identified, which are of course always perfectly understandable. He acknowledges how busy we are with our research and other duties. That day, however – and he said it surprisingly directly, in non-Uriah mode – it was my fault. What mortified me, was that he was right.

We run a couple of Access to Teaching courses with neighbouring Further Education (FE) colleges. By and large they work very well and many students have come through them successfully and gone on to obtain good degrees. Though targeted at the recruitment of students from ethnic minorities, the Access courses are not exclusively for them and a handful of white students have come through that route. The thoughtful, caring, student-centred decision I had taken had been to place two Access students together in the same school, with Tom, for their first experience which involved working together collaboratively in the same classroom, Tom's classroom. I had been quite proud of my decision. I had thought it would help them to overcome their inevitable nervousness and uncertainty if they knew each other already, and had struggled through the Access course together. I thought they would easily arrive at a mutual self-interest pact in the face of Tom's intrusiveness. What I had failed to check was whether this was OK by them or indeed whether their shared Access experience had tied a knot of common regard or even friendship.

I had also dismissed totally – out of long established wishy-washy liberal habit – any thought that it could make a difference that one was white and one was black. In practice they hated each other and for two years had worked quite hard on honing their enmity. Their mutual hatred was born of the very Access course I had thought of as a bond, and the racial tension between them was tangible. I had put two other students in the school on this placement. Both were eighteen-year-olds straight from school. Perhaps I should have put one of them with Paula and the other with Yvette – though previous experience had taught us that mature/non-mature combinations often cause conflicts and tension too. Tom had the mixed pair, and thus the problem, but he thought he also had the solution: one of them, Paula, the white student, must go. His solution owed nothing to a sensitive analysis of the whole situation. Paula's presence was causing the problem; Paula's departure would solve the problem. It followed naturally that in his view Paula was a poor teacher – in his, experienced, view. Tom has an intuitive grasp of the concept of blaming the victim though he could never acknowledge, analyse or even recognise it. Paula must go; Yvette must stay. I had put them there. Would I please come to 'talk this through' and arrange for Paula to be removed.

Paula and Yvette were both very interesting characters and with considerable potential for teaching. Both are now approaching the final year and both could be valuable assets to the schools they join. This, however, was not always the case, as evidenced from the story of the first-year placement. Paula was one of two white students on that particular Access course. She was 27 years old at the time of my Big Mistake, on her own with two children of mixed race origin, who both attend Meadowbank Primary School in the inner city, a partnership school of our University. The Headteacher there is a part-time School Experience tutor and frequent visiting lecturer for both Initial Teacher Education (ITE) and Continuing Professional Development (CPD) courses.

Paula has certainly experienced the hardships of life. Her own childhood was spent in a poor, fatherless family where she had to fight for mental survival and for the opportunity to continue her education. As a result of these circumstances, she joined us with a rather aggressive – as opposed to assertive – approach to life. She was known to be outspoken, often loud and frequently argumentative. The Headteacher of her childrens' school, where she has been a regular parental helper, had previously advised us that she was likely to dramatise situations and to escalate confrontation between parents and sometimes children. Because her partner left her without any financial support, she had very negative feelings towards men. She had a great desire to be a teacher, and from the outset thought she knew a great deal about teaching from her experience in Meadowbank School and from bringing up her children, mostly on her own. She remained consistently dismissive of the younger students on the course, especially the women.

'They don't know what real life is all about,' she said to me once. 'All they've done is go to school and get a few A levels. All they're interested in is having a good time, and finding a boyfriend'.

Yvette was about Paula's age and had lived locally all her life, though she had always had very strong links with her parents' families in Jamaica. She no longer lived at home. Since taking the Access course she had moved in with two girls whom she met on our course, the other two in fact who had been placed at Tom's school, although not in Tom's care.

Doing the Access course had been a big decision for Yvette. She had had to work very hard to convince her parents that it would be worthwhile. Before doing the course Yvette had worked with young adults with special educational needs in a day centre. This had given her some experience of educational contexts, and she was keen to teach in a special school once she was qualified. She had little experience of young children, only the few weeks she had spent on attachment to her local primary school in inner-city Manchester. She had enjoyed this, especially working with black children and helping them 'to know more about their heritage'. Yvette had become very involved with anti-racist work and frequently wrote short pieces for the local newsletter of the black community. She was articulate, albeit a little prone to aggressive, polemical and overtly political monologues. She and Paula had had a number of confrontations, both since joining the course and previously on the Access course. This, of course, I found out after my Big Mistake.

It was with some feeling of drowning, not waving, that I arrived at the school, and put my head round the office door. I knew the head teacher well, as will become clear. He knew all about Tom, but Tom had been very keen to participate in the new school-based training, whereas most of the staff had been sceptical. Tom had been one of the four to volunteer and the most up-front of those, so his offer was graciously accepted by his head teacher who came straight to the point with me: 'You've made a real pig's ear of this one, haven't you?'

We exchanged pleasantries and I discovered a gleam of light. He was unaware of Tom's solution to show Paula the red card.

'Nonsense, get on with it ... learn to work together ... can't be doing with tantrums ... she seems a good teacher to me, and if anyone makes this silly fuss into a racial incident, I have to fill in fifty forms and a man from the offices comes down mob-handed. Sort it out or never darken my doorstep again.'

Or words to that effect. At least I had something.

Fortunately, I was able to find Tom, alone and free, and we found a quiet corner of the resources room where he promised we wouldn't be disturbed. He wasted not a moment before sketching out Paula's deficiencies, interspersed with a number of comments about the weaknesses of any admissions procedure which could admit her as a trainee to the profession. In vain did I point out the obvious.

'Tom,' I said, 'like all applicants Paula was interviewed according to a procedure which always involves a head teacher from a partner school, or a senior experienced professional – a mentor like you.'

My protestations fell on deaf ears. According to Tom, Paula was the pits, rough, even uncouth, in speech, ungrammatical, uncooperative, arrogant, abrasive, quarrelsome and racist. He asserted that she had badly upset Yvette with whom she was paired. Tom clearly liked Yvette. I was soon to find out why.

Meantime, I felt I had to attempt some reconstruction of Paula. I tackled the issue of racism head on. I explained how I felt that such an allegation did not fit with Paula's own background.

'It doesn't make sense, Tom,' I said, 'Paula may have split up with her black partner, but with two mixed-race children to shepherd through the education system, she is hardly likely to be overtly racist.'

In any case, I harboured some doubts about Yvette, who had already shown herself to be aggressively anti-racist, quick to take offence at all kinds of actions and events which she interpreted as racist. I pursued Tom on this and somewhat reluctantly he did progressively concede that the interpretation of Paula's disagreements with Yvette as racist owed much to the spin which Yvette put on the events. However we quickly turned to the heart of the quarrel. As explained, Paula and Yvette were then in their first year of the BEd degree. The school experience scheme required a school to accept four students – two 'pairs' – each pair working with a teacher–tutor mentor and each teacher–tutor cross-moderating the other's students. This was intended to bring about a somewhat artificial separation between the deep involvement of professional development through mentoring and the more objective processes involving assessment of progress.

In my experience teacher–tutor mentors often develop close empathies with their students which can often get in the way of making more objective judgements. Moreover, paired working is all very well and splendid for developing collaboration and honing one's interpersonal skills, but bits fall off it when each individual in the pair hates the other. They had fallen out on this occasion over the choice of a biographical study which formed part of the Victorian Britain Key Stage 2 History Unit.

Tom had made it absolutely clear, as he assured me he always does, that the choice of 'life' to be studied was up to the two students. He had also explained that if they wanted to choose Florence Nightingale, then he would be happy to make available to them his own lesson plans, notes, resources and worksheets, together with a video compiled from a BBC programme. But it was their choice. Yvette had thought Tom's idea was an excellent one, that they were very lucky to have so helpful a mentor, that they could learn a lot from using his material and resources and that the time saved could be devoted to energising their teaching. Yvette was openly grateful to Tom for his kindness. Yvette is no mug. Surprisingly – or should that be unsurprisingly – Paula saw things differently. If they were going to look at the Crimean War, its conditions and impact on nursing, then they should break out of the traditional stereotypical framework and introduce the children to the life and times of the other great achiever in medicine and nursing, Mary Seacole, who just happened to be black and of Jamaican origin, whereas Florence Nightingale was a standard, romanticised, white middle-class heroine. In Paula's view, Yvette was betraying her heritage and selling out to conventional white anglo-centric values for reasons which were obvious.

'Yvette is a creep and a lazy cow,' she said to me, a touch unprofessionally. Yvette had of course been happy to present an alternative picture.

She ranted, 'We all know about Mary Seacole don't we? She was only cited in the original, pre-Dearing revision as a sop to ethnicity and then she was dropped. Do her if you want but don't imagine she's important.' This was the way Yvette interpreted the requirement. 'Pupils should be taught about the lives of men, women and children at different levels of society in Britain.'

'In any case,' she added, 'Mary Seacole was an Uncle Tom (there appeared to be no feminist equivalent) from a rich mulatto family – an élitist snob with appallingly racist views about native Americans'

To listen to Yvette was to learn that Mary Seacole was a woman grown rich on the profits of slavery and the excesses of Empire who had conned for herself a handful of medals, a wealth of publicity and a consequent whipround which had taken her to higher levels still of fame and prosperity. To maintain that such a character was, in any way, a role model for black, working-class women was ridiculous. She might well be a role model for individuals of mixed race, ducking and diving to 'belong' to two cultures neither of which was properly theirs. Yvette's assumption, which she made explicit, was that herein lay the appeal for Paula.

Tom didn't want to get involved in all this. He just thought that it would have been nice if they could both have gone along with his materials on Florence Nightingale. He didn't have any materials on Mary Seacole and he tended to agree with Yvette's interpretation of why she had been demoted in the official National Curriculum documents.

'As far as I'm concerned,' said Tom, 'Paula was just being awkward in a rude, rough and aggressive way.'

It is true that Paula's speech demonstrates strong regional and local characteristics and that common usage predominates. It is a little rough and ready and her voice is not harmonious. However, her written work is remarkably accurate, and I showed this to Tom. I used her file, drawing to his attention the fact that he had already perused it in great detail without finding cause for concern. In terms of the spoken word, Paula certainly fell below Level 7 of the National Curriculum in English, but the children in the class not only understood her but identified with her. Beyond that she was strong, and when Tom and I dipped into the children's written work, we found that she had been consistently conscientious in correcting grammatical errors. In fact, Paula was a relatively high achiever in terms of her personal knowledge about language. So, in the end, it all came down to the fact that she hadn't gone along with Tom's clear, if superficially masked, belief that she should have followed his ideas. And in the process she had fallen out loudly, abusively and aggressively with Yvette. Yvette had clearly managed to wind her up about the matter and had provoked Paula to the point where she had forcibly expressed her opinions in front of the children.

By now Tom was backing off.

'Derek is quite a supporter of Paula, you know,' I had pointed out to him. 'He thinks it's all a lot of fuss about nothing.'

Tom's modified view was now clear. It was up to me to sort it out. He felt that as a mentor his role was professional development. There were clearly personal issues and he simply didn't want to get involved. Tom had been on a mentor preparation course and he had certainly absorbed the messages about drawing a clear line between professional and personal issues. Personal matters were for the University to sort out. It was down to me and he would go along with whatever I decided.

I recognised that I had a number of matters concerning professional behaviour and professionalism which I needed to explore between Paula and Yvette. I decided that I had to know a lot more about what had gone on in the Access course and whether there were other things going on, now that both of them had joined the BEd course and someone had thoughtfully placed them together in their first school experience programme. I decided to strike while the iron was hot and speak to the students there and then in school, first on their own and then together. We retreated to the resources room.

Paula was openly hostile in her demeanour, adopting an aggressive body stance. When asked to sit down, she did so grudgingly, reluctant to make eye contact, and gave off a 'don't think I'm going to change my mind about this one' attitude.

I took a deep breath.

'OK – let's have it from the beginning then – what's all this about? And before you begin can I remind you that I look to you to be thoroughly professional in your discussion of this matter'.

That seemed to take the wind out of her sails – she had expected me to launch straight in to my best lecture on behaving professionally – but I was saving that for later! Paula explained how, right from the word go, she and Yvette had not got on when joining the Access course. Paula had found the coursework to be easily within her ability, unlike Yvette, who struggled to keep up with the rest. Paula had on occasion been a little smug about her achievements (she admitted she might even have publicly commented on this). She had such an overtly 'if you've got it, flaunt it' sort of approach, that I could read what had gone on.

The situation had got worse over the year on the Access course, Yvette using her popularity with the other members of the course to get them to isolate Paula and to make her so miserable that she felt like giving up. There had been many arguments about anti-racist issues, in which Yvette always took the opposite view from Paula, and this current situation seemed to Paula like a bigger version of the skirmishes of last year. Yvette, who now shared a house with the other two students in the school, had managed to turn both of them against her, which had led to a terrible atmosphere. She was hurt and upset about Tom's attitude.

'He hasn't given me a fair chance. He's always siding with Yvette, because she curried favour with him by agreeing with everything he suggested.'

By this time Paula had well and truly worked herself up into a highly agitated state and I recognised the need to calm her down and try to find a possible way forward, so that some semblance of professional behaviour might be restored. I decided to talk about children and their entitlement to a fair deal. I knew Paula had a very strong commitment to this. She had fought many a battle for her own two children, and she was known as something of a champion of children's rights.

'How do you feel you came across to the children, Paula, when you exploded at Yvette? Is that the kind of role model you want for the children? What would your response be if children openly squabbled and abused each other in the classroom?'

Moving from children's entitlement on to student entitlement, I made the connections between helping children resolve their conflicts and having to take a professional approach to colleagues. By this time Paula was looking a bit sheepish, and I asked her to take some time to think, not only about the implications of her behaviour, but also the irony of having a mentor call in a tutor to sort out a fracas between two students. I asked her to try to write about the incident in a professional way, trying to analyse the events so as to help her develop her professional awareness, as an entry for her file. I emphasised the need to avoid emotive or judgmental language.

After telling her that I would speak with Yvette, then meet both of them together, and emphasising the seriousness of the situation, I saw her wipe a tear away from her eye.

'Will this incident affect my School Experience assessment?'

I considered my reply and said that if a 'professional ' way of redeeming the situation could be achieved, and suitable reflection and evaluation of behaviour and strategies developed for the future identified, we could probably say that a steep learning curve had been experienced in the area of professional awareness and interpersonal skills.

Paula understands both the nuances of language and the importance of negotiation. I noticed a visible lightening of her face and felt somewhat reassured as to the possible outcome of events. As we walked out of the resources room, I made a mental note of thanks to those tutors who had argued so strongly for the inclusion of Professional Awareness when we were having one of the many discussions about the new TTA criteria for the assessment of teaching. Was I glad that we had resisted the push to go down a simplistic competences-driven model and still had some holistic and flexible criteria with which to assess students!

But, next . . . Yvette. I was not looking forward to this as, on arrival, I had caught a glimpse of Yvette's tearstained face in the staffroom, before my conversation with Paula. I had been the recipient of a look from her which caused me to wish I was not the white middle class tutor I inevitably was. I re-entered the resources room in which I had now spent some two hours discussing and negotiating.

Yvette looked at me with some hostility.

'I suppose you are going to tell me off and fail me on my teaching practice, just because I've had a showdown with her,' she offered as an opening gambit.

I obviously took her by surprise when I asked if I could look at her justifications for her History topic planning and asked her to talk me through the rationale for using Florence Nightingale rather than Mary Seacole as a focus for nursing in the Crimean War. I did stress that I was a specialist History tutor with a particular interest in Black History, and understood her lack of experience of the History curriculum, due to the fact that any input on History for non-specialists did not occur until Year 2 of the BEd degree. I also gave her the standard little spiel about talking about colleagues in a professional way and referred to the lengthy discussions about the need for effective professional relationships which had occurred in Extended Professional Studies sessions.

She took quite a long time to respond to my request and if her facial expressions were anything to go by, she was having quite an internal debate about how to respond. Eventually, she did concede that there was no reason not to present a variety of viewpoints in History. More importantly, I drew from her an account of the skills that children needed to develop which included those of questioning, analysis, critical appraisal, information retrieval, documentary source analysis and techniques in gathering data through oral history. She had a fair grasp of what she was about. Having established a dialogue with her I asked her to explain the interpersonal problems between her and Paula, reminding her of the need to be professional (I was beginning to wince at the word) at all times, and to use appropriate language. Choosing her words carefully, Yvette went through the problems experienced during the Access course, but slipped up when she talked about Paula's excellent work. She made it quite obvious that she thought Paula's partner, who turned out to be an ex-boyfriend of Yvette's sister – wheels within wheels – had helped her a great deal with her written work. My pointing out that Paula was now on her own and still producing excellent work seemed to upset Yvette, and she began to sob and complain about how she found the coursework difficult. After calming her down with promises of tutorial help and guidance, I tackled her about her unacceptable behaviour and asked her to write a brief entry for her file, which I would read in draft, and give her help with.

'Let's call it a day now,' I said, 'and the three of us will sit down in college tomorrow and sort it out.' An evil thought came into my mind, 'Why don't you chat it over with Tom?' I suggested, as I made my way out.

Next day, back at college, Paula and Yvette were in my room, allegedly neutral territory. I embarked on my standard 'professional behaviour' lecture. I can mount a high horse with the best of them!

I worked my way through the standard precepts: the need to accept differences – to be flexible – to present a role model for children – to find ways of asking questions rather than making negative statements, and more. I informed them that I expected them to liaise with me fully, and to outline how they had resolved their conflict. I required them to team-teach the History sessions and evaluate them carefully, using Tom. I also requested them to present a case study of their conflict for their first session of Extended Professional Studies, on their return to university following the end of the placement. I marvelled inwardly at my skills in dealing with difficult situations involving interpersonal relationships. Not for nothing had I been on counselling courses!

There still remained Tom. Somehow I would have to enlist his support. Without his cooperation, the 'deal' wouldn't work. The following week I returned to the school and sought him out. I have been a little critical of Tom, I know, but he is keen and, although blinkered and all the other things I have called him, he is not stupid. I decided that there was only one course of action. I told him the absolute truth as I saw it, even to the point of explaining that Paula saw him as playing favourites. To soften the blow, I freely acknowledged my error in setting up that particular placement. He nodded vigorously but accepted that we all now needed his help to get Paula out of the fine mess I had got her in to. I explained that Paula too recognised that much fault lay with her, particularly in her attitude. But, as I stressed, she now needed help. It was no good removing her from the placement. She had to deal with the situation. He was her mentor and she had to work through it with him. The team-teaching, I stressed, would require challenging support from him. Could he and I crack the problem . . . together? You bet we could!

The team-teaching wasn't brilliant. Tom kept a tight rein on everything and was too prescriptive to allow much room for creativity, but in the circumstances his approach served its purpose. Paula was glad to be included. Yvette was relieved not to be excluded. Neither was anxious to test herself again, either against each other or individually. Tom offered certainty in a world which had appeared to be falling apart. What they learnt about teaching and learning was very limited. What they learnt about interpersonal relationships and the significance of 'professional awareness' was to stand them in good stead, I felt sure.

I met the headteacher again soon after.

'See,' he said, 'just like I told you and Tom – a lot of fuss about nothing – it just needed a firm hand. Good chap Tom. Manages to rub along with all you busybody tutors'.

COMMENTARY AND MATTERS FOR DISCUSSION

The importance of context

The placement of students in school is often a delicate operation, and the issue of context recurs in Chapter 6, 'Debriefing: triumph and disaster'. Paula's tale touches on some of the dangers. Issues of compatibility and the ability to behave appropriately in sometimes hostile environments can stretch the emerging professionalism of students and expose weaknesses in the mentoring and tutoring processes. A good account from the USA is to be found in *Emerging as a Teacher* Bullough, Knowles and Crow (1991), while Thompson (1997) contributes a useful paper to the discussion of professional ethics and the teaching profession. The tale also is cautionary in that it highlights the danger of making superficially attractive assumptions, e.g. Access students might like to carry on working together. The real problem lies in the fact that, whatever they might sometimes think, tutors sit outside the circle of knowledge of what is really happening within the student population. The moral of this tale might well be that placement officers should just get on and do their job to consistent rules and stop deluding themselves. The bits of knowledge they have may be little more than gossip and then only a fraction of the truth. As to 'matching' students, there is an argument that eventually fate will land them in a staffroom or paired with a colleague quite different from what they would have wanted, and the sooner they learn to deal with it the better. Paula and Yvette, despite appropriate preparation, struggled to come to terms with being thrown into a new and challenging situation, namely, 'a real teacher's classroom' at an early stage of their careers.

Guests and their gifts

Both Paula and Yvette are 'guests'. The feeling of being a guest in someone else's classroom or school is discussed by Edwards in Edwards and Collison (1996). She argues that such a feeling is not always helpful to students in gaining access to the complex web of relationships, routines and norms of individual primary schools. However, guests often bring 'gifts' of their own specialist expertise or make time for teachers to spend with individual pupils. Unfortunately, in this tale, Paula's good knowledge of History is not used and the disagreements between the pair use up much of Tom's time, to the point where he becomes exasperated, loses his sense of proportion and seeks to act irrationally. A guest situation can prove problematic for those students at the very beginning of their course, who have not yet recognised or discovered their special 'gifts'. The terminology suggests a power relationship between host and guest, rather than a perhaps more conducive, collaborative partnership which is built upon mutual respect, self-appraisal and the giving and receiving of constructive feedback.

Cultural pressures

Paula and Yvette were not attuned to the ethos of Jemima Johnston Primary School. Aspects of the culture of a primary school and their effects on student–mentor relationships are documented in Campbell and Kane's (1996a) analysis of mentoring in primary schools. The pressure on students to conform to the behavioural, attitudinal and social norms of the school can often result in students taking up offers they should refuse, such as those of Tom, resulting in lesson plans and exact copies of sessions run by the mentor. It is worth debating how far this is helpful to the student and how far it is an impediment to development.

Micro-politics

The tension between supporting and challenging students is a complex issue, which, as a theme, will be returned to several times in our tales. When taken in the context of the micro-politics of many schools it becomes a minefield for students trying to establish and develop themselves as teachers, see Hoyle (1982) and Sparkes and Mackay (1996). Tom's reaction to the conflict between Paula and Yvette, to blame one of them and to favour the other, is one which puts a student in a difficult position, as an unwanted 'guest' who has little negotiating power. Comparable issues emerge in Sharon's story (Chapter 4) and are discussed there. One thing the tale does illustrate is how a situation can be observed and described in widely varied ways by different individuals (the narrator, the head teacher, Tom, Paula and Yvette). It is also the case that the same individual will give different descriptions according to the audience.

Roles and responsibilities

The role of the university tutor, as perceived by Tom, namely, that of the 'fire brigade member' or 'troubleshooter', is one commonly fallen back on by teachers when the problems become difficult or complex, see Campbell and Kane (1996a) and Fish (1995b). Much thought arguably needs to be given to 'separate but equal' roles in partnerships for schools and higher education. The two roles can usefully come together through joint supervision and assessment of students. The work of Furlong *et al.* (1996) discusses this 'separation' and 'division of labour' in so-called 'collaborative' models of partnership and raises important issues of power and control.

Support or challenge?

This issue will recur in the tales. There is an interesting debate to be had about how to encourage autonomy and critical appraisal of practice. Is such an arrangement feasible as an ongoing event or does it represent little more than a useful approach to mentor preparation? Biott and Spindler (1995) comment on the need for higher education staff to help schools work out ways for students to manage their participation in daily school life so as to enhance their learning opportunities. The foregoing scenario illustrates just how difficult that can be and why establishing effective and facilitative relationships between staff in schools and universities is a necessary and vital component of school-based training. In their study of mentors, Cameron-Jones and O'Hara (1997) identify the presence of, and personal preference for, support rather than challenge. As will be seen from later discussion, Dunne and Bennett (1997) disagree with this position.

Cloning

The issue of mentors wanting to clone students in their own style of teaching, and consequently putting pressure on students, is common but is one which could well reduce with the progressive development of school-based training. One of the advantages which university tutors had in the old system of touring supervision was that they frequently encountered a variety of contexts and models of teaching. By contrast classroom teachers, while having the clear advantage of knowing the specific context in which a student was teaching, had relatively little else – other than self – as a basis for comparison. One of the important lessons to be learned through mentor training and preparation is the need to stress the dangers of cloning, and one of the best ways to do this is through a selection of contrasting teaching styles portrayed on film and video. Less efficient, but arguably more effective, is the exchange of teachers as mentors, which can be within a school but, better still, between schools.

Other issues

Most of the above issues have been introduced briefly and will recur. Some will need to be explored in considerable detail. However, the tale sets down markers for a number of other issues which can all be found to relate directly or indirectly to school-based training.

- Interpersonal relationships: the bag incidents and invasion of privacy
- Mentor selection: who does it and how?
- Avoiding school–Higher Education (HE) rivalries. Do partnerships herald the end of the 'forget everything they taught you at college' syndrome?
- Stances on Equal Opportunities issues: What happens if the student is the conscience? Should the mentor follow even if this conflicts with school practice and/or private belief?
- Mentor detachment: the avoidance of personal involvement – keeping a distance. How much distance?
- Mature students: are there 'special needs' implications for mentoring mature students, or are all students the same?
- What is subject knowledge? For example 'knowledge about language': do schools, especially primary schools, have the skills to remediate subject knowledge weaknesses? Paula had more 'knowledge about language' than Tom, seemingly:
- Negotiation: the avoidance of absolutes in mentoring, and leaving room for manoeuvre. Head teachers and experienced tutors seem able to sort things out usually. Does wisdom come with age or do they actually duck the real issues, dealing only with the short-term problems while leaving the long-term issues unaddressed? How long will school-based training prosper on a grace-and-favour basis?

FURTHER READING

For discussion about challenge and support in school-based teacher education see the following:

Cameron-Jones, M. and O'Hara, P. (1997) 'Support and challenge in teacher education', *British Educational Research Journal* **23**(1), 15–26.
Dunne, E. and Bennett, N. (1997) 'Mentoring processes in school-based training', *British Educational Research Journal* **23**(2), 225–37.

Primary school culture is discussed in the following:

Campbell, A. and Kane, I. (1996) 'Mentoring and primary school culture', in McIntyre, D. and Hagger, H. (eds) *Mentors in Schools: Developing the Profession of Teaching*. London: David Fulton Publishers.
Crowther, G. (1995) 'A primary school view of involvement in initial teacher training', in Bines, H. and Welton, J. M. (eds) *Managing Partnership in Teacher Training and Development*. London: Routledge.

Discussion of schools in collaboration with Higher Education can be located in:

Edwards, A. (1996) 'Making the most of relationships with Higher Education', in Edwards, A. and Collison, J. *Mentoring and Developing Practice in Primary Schools.* Milton Keynes: Open University Press.
Furlong, J. *et al.* (1996) 'Redefining partnership: revolution or reform in initial teacher education?' *Journal of Education for Teaching* **22**(1), 39–55.

For an in depth examination of equality issues see:

Richardson, R. (1990) *Daring to be a Teacher.* Stoke-on-Trent: Trentham Books.

A discussion of professionalism and professional ethics is well presented in:

Thompson, M. (1997) *Professional Ethics and the Teacher; towards a General Teaching Council.* Stoke-on-Trent: Trentham Books.

CHAPTER 2

The meeting: staff, parents and governors

I drove away reflectively. The spat between Paula and Yvette was pretty well the only problematic situation which we had encountered in the first year of our partnership. My mind flashed back to the day eighteen months previously when I had presented the case for partnership to the uncertain staff and governors . . .

I was experiencing mixed feelings about the meeting which I was scheduled to attend at the Jemima Johnston Primary School as I made my way there to arrive shortly before the end of the day. It wasn't the first such meeting I'd done since, at the travelling road show, Our Leader had promised, 'If you want someone to come and talk to the staff and/or the governors, you have only to ask and we will be there.'

It was a necessary, important promise but unfortunately it has lost something in the translation. For 'we' read 'I'. This was my fifth. I was beginning to know my lines. A word about the travelling road show . . . . When it became clear that 'partnership' with secondary schools, launched in 1992, and working pretty well as far as I could see, was going to have to be extended to primary schools, we had taken it upon ourselves to set up half a dozen meetings for primary school heads, or their nominees. Two were at base, on our campus. One was by day for those who complained that 'after school' meetings made a long day longer; one was in the evening, to meet the wishes of those heads who felt that neither they nor a deputy could or should leave the school. The latter position wins my respect but I always felt that it didn't augur well for persuading schools to take on major new responsibilities for training students. In any case, many of the heads, teachers and schools seemed pretty spaced out to me. Barely recovered from the national curriculum in its several forms, contemplating the financial problems induced by LMS and beginning to see the massed hordes of OFSTED appearing on the horizon, several were in shock. That could lead to resistance. Equally it could lead to a shrug of shoulders and, 'What's one more reform, anyway?' A delightful, constructive approach, in my view.

The other four meetings were held at venues roughly corresponding to the four main points of the compass, with our campus at the centre, in a mixture of lunchtime, afternoon and evening, and of teachers' days and 'real time'. They were distributed in that pattern largely for the benefit of those participants who figured our campus was too far, or couldn't make the actual dates chosen. Anyone could go anywhere, at any time, once, twice or to all six if they rated the entertainment value. We provided quite generous hospitality, using money from the TTA to be used for promoting partnership. It was always necessary to explain that it was 'central' money intended for that purpose. In our experience the provision of hospitality was a two-edged sword. Lots of participants had had to rush to attend and deserved a decent tea or coffee and something to eat. At the same time, if the fare on offer was too obviously a couple of Michelin rosettes above the school kitchen, the staffroom microwave, or the local sandwich bar, then we were in danger of conveying the impression that higher education was awash with money. That would have been a big mistake, particularly since what we were trying to persuade schools to do was potentially to take on new work and responsibilities for not much financial reward. I knew for sure that this issue would come up at the meeting. I reckoned that by now I knew the questions and I knew the answers. My problem was that, even in my opinion, the answers were pretty unsatisfactory.

There was, however, one area of uncertainty about this particular meeting. This was the first time that the head of a school had taken up the option of extending the invitation to members of his governing body. This head, Derek Wilson, was a former MEd student. My guess was that he was going to be supportive.

'You don't mind do you?' he'd said, as he introduced me to the three people who were sitting in his room as I arrived. 'This is Dr Noble, our chair of governors. Her day job is registrar at our local hospital.'

I mentally noted that 'our local hospital' happens to be one of the six largest in the UK.

'This is Mrs Craven, a parent governor and ward sister at the hospital.'

I'd got the message. There were two there from the health service and my forthcoming explanations (excuses?) about the impoverished state of higher education would be understood, but there would be a cutting edge to some of the questions and it would not be possible to seek the sympathy vote. The third governor was introduced as Councillor Didcot, one of the LEA representatives.

'I used to come here as a lad,' he told me. 'I've seen the school go through many changes, but I never thought I'd see it doing the work of the local university,' he continued with a laugh. Well, it seemed like a laugh.

We made our way to the staffroom where the assembled throng was waiting, if nineteen can be adjudged a throng.

'I'll do the introductions,' said Derek. 'We've got an open mind on what you'll be suggesting; some of my colleagues are quite keen on the idea, and the rest might well be happy to let them get on with it, as long as the "mentoring" ... (have I got the term right?) ... doesn't interfere with the real work of the classes.'

'Oh well,' I thought, 'so much for the concept of the mentoring school. I might have a little difficulty with that one. Still they've asked me here, some of them are keen, and I know a couple of them well. The governors seem on the ball, and they're interested enough to come. All in all, I think I'm on promising ground.'

The head proceeded with his introductions.

'This is Wilma Hudson, Deputy Head, whom I know you are well acquainted with from your MEd course. Next to her is Meg White, Head of Early Years. You might have met Tom Smith before, I think. He's had many students through his hands in the past. Joan Scott is Wilma's next door neighbour in the classroom sense and they team up quite a lot. Over there is Mark Bennet who has only just joined us here at Jemima Johnston Primary School. And last but not least, there's Damien Karcewski. He's new to the school and to mentoring but very keen to get started, and he's waiting in the wings, as it were.'

All the foregoing were to have parts, large or small, to play in the events which were to unfold over the next three or four years of school-based training. The other teachers and assistants were to serve as backdrop, as 'extras', but as Derek ran through the introductions I knew none of this. In any case at that time, all I wanted to do was begin the meeting proper.

'So that's us, and we know you. You're the one who twists our arm to take students on teaching practice.'

'School experience,' I murmured.

'And now you want us to tutor them as well. I reckon we can't do worse than some of your gang. The last one we had was right off the wall. He said he was a post-modernist and was trying to open up the student's view of the classroom. It seems he reckoned his job was to be like that little French devil Asmodé who flew around at night, lifting the lids of houses to see what was going on. If that's the job, then I reckon we can do that, and while we're at it, we might show them how to teach reading. Your post-modernist guy hadn't a clue. Still I mustn't rabbit on, it's not my meeting, so over to you.'

By now, having done several of these sessions, I had worked out my spiel, which was how I was coming to think of it. I knew the hostages to fortune, the traps and the pitfalls. I also knew that there was a strong chance of walking right into them. I decided against early jokes – straight into the business.

'Thank you for asking me,' I began. 'I hope this is the start of a genuine partnership. Yes, you know me as the placement tutor and troubleshooter, but the whole point of my being here is to explain that my role, like yours, will have to change if we are to make our partnership work.'

A few heads nodded. I relaxed a little.

'My job today is to tell you about recent government proposals for change in the way primary teachers are to be trained. These changes follow two years behind other changes in secondary education, which are now well-established.

You may be familiar with the main outlines of what has been happening, leading up to the Official Circular, which has been sent to all schools, Circular 14/93. However, you could have missed a twist or a turn, so I'd like to give you a brief update on the current situation and raise some issues that have emerged.'

So far they seemed attentive. A couple were taking notes. This could be OK.

'Briefly, from 1994 all *secondary* teacher training had to be revised to take account of new criteria issued by the Secretary of State. Students now spend more time in schools which have forged partnership agreements with institutions of higher education; schools have taken over more responsibility for training; the extent to which their responsibility has increased varies from school to school and from training institution to training institution, depending on the nature of what is called the partnership agreement; money is changing hands. The main areas in which schools are expected to have an enlarged role are in the supervision and assessment of the practice of teaching, and the delivery of certain sorts of professional knowledge which beginning teachers need to have. Collaboration is now more formalised and the concept of mentoring has become central. I need to explain the statutory framework of change.'

I didn't really, but I didn't want them to think this was something we had dreamed up on our own. So I embarked on a rapid tour of recent change.

'The new criteria for secondary changes were issued in July of 1992, via Circular 9/92. The criteria are actually the Secretary of State's criteria but are more usually called the CATE criteria. CATE is the Council for the Accreditation of Teacher Education – the body which for over ten years has directed teacher training. Circular 9/92 was actually CATE 3. CATE 1 was in 1984, CATE 2 in 1989. Its author was the self-declared hero of education – and founding father of the National Curriculum – Kenneth Baker. CATE 4 "The Sequel – Primary Education", is what has just reached us, and it has to be implemented by 1996. There will not be a CATE 5. The new Education Act has killed it.'

I could see that the crack about Kenneth Baker and the National Curriculum had begun to pull them on my side. They were probably thinking that anyone who could be rude about Kenneth Baker could not be all bad. Time now to talk about what really mattered to them.

'Some aspects of the new arrangements are likely to be similar in the primary training development, but there are likely to be some very significant differences. Major similarities include the involvement of schools in the planning and delivery of the courses; a significant role in the supervision and assessment of students; and the transfer of funding to underwrite work previously done by Higher Education, but which will in future be done by schools.'

From now on, in my limited experience, it would be uphill, then downhill.

'What are the differences?' I asked.

I had every intention of telling them, and worked my way through the obvious, such as time, usage, PGCE/BEd variations and so on. The next bit was a little tricky. Somehow we had to establish that this was going to be a real partnership, when several people there didn't want it to be, and others feared it wasn't going to be. They thought it would be the same old master–slave relationship. Old wine in new bottles.

'You can assume willingness on our part to move in new directions. In the last few years it has been as though two different versions of the same plot were running at the same time.'

By now I was well into my stride. I needed to make them understand as well that we were going into partnerships with a positive attitude.

'I'll shorthand the two plots: the HMI version and the Kenneth Clarke version.'

I sensed a *frisson* of approval: this tutor talking to them was hostile to Kenneth Clarke as well as Kenneth Baker. So I warmed to my task.

'The HMI version was this "Brown Book".'

I held up a copy of the HMI Report on School-Based Initial Training, published the same day as Clarke had given his Southport speech in January 1992.

'The new arrangements which have evolved are in practice very close to this HMI version, but what is often remembered is the rhetoric of Kenneth Clarke's speech at the North of England Conference.'

I could have sworn someone hissed.

'This has caused a great deal of confusion. So – a word about confusions.'

I was going now into territory that had seemed to matter a lot to secondary heads and their senior staff. I wasn't sure that it was the main item on primary schools' agenda.

'There was initially, post-Clarke, publicity about schools being in the lead. This was good rhetoric but when schools in a scheme disagreed, which school was to be in the lead? The emphasis quickly shifted to Partnership. In Partnership, Higher Education will retain responsibility for the students who are registered for an award and will continue to be on a BEd or PGCE course, as now. Higher Education receives funding for those students, but passes part of it to schools when it is agreed who does what.'

'How much?' said a voice from the body of the staff.

'An important question,' I said, 'a crucial question and I promise you I will come to it, but let me just develop my theme.'

Now I was coming to the bit which I felt confident about.

'Originally, training was going to be only in secondary schools of the highest standard, schools which could achieve high quality performance indicators; the very best A Levels, the best SATs results, high staying-on rates, low truancy rates, good inspection reports. This was quickly shown to be impractical, élitist nonsense.'

'I should think so,' said a voice. Meg, I think it was. 'They need a mixed diet'. This commanded general support, so I continued.

'The Clarke speech envisaged a much smaller number of schools being involved while taking a larger number of students, ten to twelve. Although involvement on this scale is certainly not now excluded, it will be the exception not the rule, and most secondary schools seem more comfortable with between four and six – throughout much of the year. You may think *that* sounds a lot.'

They did.

'One thing which was quite new in Circular 9/92, has remained unaltered throughout the consultative process, and is present in the Primary Circular 14/93, is the shift to outcome criteria.'

'What's that when it's translated from education-speak?' asked the same voice who had asked about money.

'By outcome criteria,' I replied, 'I mean the specification of those competences appropriate to a beginning teacher.'

I was conscious that I had not reduced the jargon level.

'Earlier arrangements for teacher training were concerned with input criteria. The Secretary of State via the DES (as was) specified what had to be done in a course of initial training. Sometimes they specified the actual hours to be allocated to course components. Now, the *finishing line* is what is identified. How students arrive there is for partners, Higher Education and schools, collectively, to determine – and to show how it has been done. As an aside, there is a very important potential link here with career entry profiles for NQTs.'

I knew the school has done a lot of work on profiling generally, and was good on structured support for its NQTs.

'Quality control will be via HMI inspection.'

I saw them wince. They thought I meant them. I plunged recklessly on about arguments concerning linking funding to quality. Little did I know quite how elaborate the inspection system would prove to be, nor how much of a nightmare the combined efforts of the TTA and OFSTED to justify their respective roles in the quality industry would have to be endured, nor how OFSTED inspection would disrupt and damage partnerships. All that lay in the future. I could have done with Mystic Meg. In my naivety, I continued optimistically.

'I must repeat that we are not talking about old wine in new bottles. 1996, the target start date for full implementation (How was I to know that before long we would have Circular 10/97 and new rules?) should see new-style courses, requiring a major reconceptualisation by Higher Education and schools of who does what. The shift to outcome criteria and profiling are examples that there is a new job to be done, which has still to be defined.'

In front of me several eyes were glazing over. The LEA governor's body language was now also signalling 'jargon', 'claptrap', 'education-speak'. I continued, a touch pompously, to what I knew was the heart of what we were going to have to get involved with.

'Undoubtedly, central to the new arrangements is the concept of mentoring, that is, teachers as mentors. In post-1994 secondary and post-1996 primary courses, experienced teachers will play a much greater role in the supervision and assessment of students; students will also be in school more and some of what they have previously done in college will now need to be done in school, monitored and mediated by mentors. We need to work this out together.'

I sensed that that notion was appreciated, but I suspected, based on earlier meetings, that some teachers whose time was precious would prefer us to tell them what we wanted them to do. If they didn't like it, *they* would tell *us*. Now came the tricky bit – no avoiding it.

'But it all takes time and time is money. There are two sorts of money. Over the next two years what is called *transitional funding* will be provided to meet the costs of making the transition to the new courses. It is used in the main to buy time, for example supply-cover costs or to meet expenses such as travel costs, as we engage together in development and preparation. That funding is finite – we will get our share according to a national formula and I'll make you one promise and that is that this money will find its way into schools for development work; it will not be swallowed up in early retirement schemes, or research funding, or Swiss bank accounts.'

So far so good.

'After 1996 when we are agreed who does what, and what it is that we have previously done which schools will then do, then we will pass to you agreed sums from our annual 'per student' income. Those arrangements will be formalised by what is commonly called a Partnership Agreement. I mentioned this earlier. We are just in the process of finalising these contracts with our secondary partnership schools. All discussions have been civilised and professional, and I want to quote to you the first principle of our Secondary Partnership Agreement. *"The Partnership acknowledges that the well-being of pupils and students in schools and colleges takes priority over all other considerations."'*

I repeated that phrase with even more emphasis.

'It will be the same with those primary schools who join us in partnership.'

'What about workload?' asked Tom Smith.

'Workload' was a big issue at the time. In fact, it was being tested in the courts.

'It's a problem,' I conceded. 'In fact, the workload issue has already invaded the new experimental school fundholding pilot schemes.'

I was referring to the new government brainwave – School Centred Initial Teacher Training (SCITT) scheme – a DIY scheme where the money for training went directly to schools, who could buy in HE expertise or not – it was up to them.

What could I say? Some teachers in that room who were to be the mentors would find it very hard work at times – another pressure. There were other associated problems which I decided to tackle head on.

'In the context of potential "staff aggro", I would stress two lessons clearly learnt so far. Quality school-based training requires a whole-school commitment; if it is "owned" by only a few, it goes sour. The second is not my business, but I pass it on from our experience with secondary schools. It is that things seem to work best when the income from participation in school-based teacher training is regarded as a whole-school resource.'

I knew the issue of money would recur, but I reckoned I also knew how it would go in the end. I was dealing with teachers here, not politicians or other unprincipled classes.

'I've come to ask you to be one of the schools to join us in Partnership in the new school-based training. However, in fairness I should conclude by quoting to you some of the reasons schools have given as to why they have decided *not* to join in Partnership schemes. Some of them may be largely secondary-school-type reasons but for what they are worth here they are.'

I read out my prepared list, interested to sense their reactions.

- 'It's not our business, it's yours, it's not broken so don't fix it' (nods),
- 'We are deep into opt-out debate, come back next year' (not us, not likely),
- 'Deficit budget, we can't move till it's sorted' ('We're in surplus,' said Councillor Didcot),
- 'We are booked for inspection soon – let's get that over with' (groans),
- 'The money on offer is not enough' (murmuring),
- 'Governors, especially parent governors, are making Neanderthal noises' (I smiled at Dr Noble and Mrs Craven. They did not smile back: their minds were clearly on the egregious John Patten),
- 'We prefer to work with another college or university' (puzzlement),
- 'We have an ideological objection to innovation overload – the last-straw syndrome' (hear, hear!),
- 'If Patten's for it, we're against it' (they laughed! I'd scored a hat-trick – Baker, Clarke *and* Patten),
- 'The Head is keen. The Senior Management Team reckons it's another of the Head's bright ideas' (another laugh!),
- 'The Senior Management Team is keen, but the Head thinks their eye is on the wrong ball' (the Head laughed),
- 'Active Union is making rumbling noises; enthusiasm for innovation not fired by recent pay rise' (voice from the body of the staff laughed),
- 'Can't think for the noise of SATs' (smiling in the aisles),
- 'Let's wait for Ron Dearing' (boring!),
- 'Mentors are finding the job too demanding in the absence of quality time to do it' (pause for thought).

I'd got some laughs and smiles out of that. I had some of them now and the rest were ready to give me a fair hearing. I approached my peroration.

'I want to conclude with a point about involvement in training the next generation. It has been said that the mark of a profession is that it takes responsibility for itself and its new members. I have sympathy with schools who stand aside and maintain that taking students damages the welfare of the pupils, but it isn't all gloomy. Do students not bring something of value to the schools they work in? And will the schools who decline to take students still continue to employ newly qualified teachers, trained on the backs of other schools? Of course they will. It has been shown recently that between 70 and 80 per cent of newly qualified teachers take up their first posts within 20 to 30 miles of where they train. It will be hard for schools to avoid the consequences of new arrangements. However, even if all that is set aside, I believe that the new arrangements offer the opportunity for professional involvement in the training process which is not only greater than in the past, but is also a fascinating and, in my judgement, rewarding and satisfying challenge. In the case of BEd students, to see the change in immature 18-year-olds to 22-year-old hardened professionals is a satisfying experience; to offer second chance or second career opportunities to mature students is very worthwhile. Of all the people I have ever worked with, no group shows a faster turnround for one's efforts than the 1-year PGCE students – from September to July you can actually see the results of your work. As you know, the majority of students meet you far more than halfway in their willingness to learn and their desire to succeed. They can enrich the schools they work in. If for no other reason, I hope and believe that enough schools will find it worthwhile becoming partners with us in these new developments.'

I'd gone on a bit long, but I'd laid the basis for referencing my answers to the anticipated questions, and I'd meant what I said at the end, quite strongly. I hope and think they recognised that I wanted them with us, genuinely.

The questions came:

- 'Will we be paid for extra duties?'
- 'Will the school be paid?'
- 'How will the payments be calculated?'
- 'Will participation be compulsory?'

And so on, covering a lot of ground from supply cover to conditions of service. I grappled as best I could with the detail but I knew, realistically, that the new school-based partnership arrangements were a 'double whammy'. Schools would receive funding which would not truly compensate them for the work they would do. Higher Education would be passing over more than it could afford. The only justification would be if between us we were to provide a better training programme for the students. Eventually I was rescued, as I knew I would be, by the professional voice which unfailingly spoke up on such occasions. This time it was Wilma, the Deputy Head.

'It's not about money, is it? At least it *shouldn't* be. It's like you said, it's about training the next generation. It's not only about students. I reckon it's about our, *my*, professional development. I reckon I can learn from working with students. I guess mentoring them will help me sharpen up my own analytical skills and my teaching. No amount of money can buy that.'

I knew then that in terms of principle, the road ahead was straightforward. Things had gone that way, more or less, in all the previous meetings, and were to go the same way in future meetings. Teachers cared – about pupils, and about other teachers. It was as simple as that.

The questions which followed were mainly of a general nature. I knew that some often recurred and they were raised that day too:

- 'Will funding match the time needed?'
- 'How long will the term of a Partnership Contract be?'
- 'Will all schools accept common responsibilities in addition to mentoring?'
- 'What criteria will be used to assess a school/mentor/classteacher suitability?'
- 'What is the Labour Party's view on school-based training? Could it all stop?'
- 'What would happen if schools all said that they did not want to be involved?'
- 'What protection would schools have from failing students?'
- 'How would moderation be achieved?'
- 'What support would schools get from the university?'
- 'What would the benefits be to avoid schools feeling used, at a time of innovation overload?'
- 'Could schools work with more than one Higher Education institution?'

I answered the questions as best I could. So much lay in the future and we would have to work it out. The important thing was that I felt that here was another school which would probably join us in partnership. We were approaching decision time. The governors were clearly key figures and I felt that the Head had been wise to include them. Partnership as a concept needed the support of governing bodies.

Councillor Didcot *was* bothered about money. It transpired that he was the Chair of the Finance Sub-Committee. I took encouragement from his general approach. At no time did he appear to see school-based training as a money-making venture. He could do the sums as well as anyone. He knew, too, that the teacher–mentors would give of their time generously, far beyond the cash reward. However, he certainly didn't want the school to lose money. He knew that students were likely to devour resources and the more time they spent in school, the more resources they would devour: paper, art materials, photocopies, printing, displays and so on. He confirmed that staff would be going to external meetings and wanted to know how their costs would be covered. He pointed out the recent refurbishment of the rather small staffroom we were in and counted out the chairs for me. He did a tour of the tea, the coffee, the biscuits. He seemed to be genuinely concerned for the teachers as well as the pupils. He requested reassurance. I gave it.

Mrs Craven was bothered about the increased impact school-based training would have on the children. She was clearly testing answers against her own children.

'These mentors,' she said, 'well, this is difficult, with everyone here and I hope they forgive me, but I know a couple of the teachers here are new, so these mentors are going to be the best – no I don't mean, best – I mean the most experienced teachers, aren't they? Those with allowances and big responsi-bilities. Take Wilma, well, she's second in command, isn't she, and she's said how she'd like to be involved and I'm sure she can teach new teachers a lot, but if she's doing that, she won't be teaching the children as much, will she, so they won't be getting as much of her, will they, they'll be getting pretty raw students. I know some of them will be good, but it's the same with trainee nurses, I've seen it on the ward. It's the poor ones who take the time. So will it affect the children's education? And I've got to say it, and I know it sounds awful, but my Jamie is going into Wilma's class next year and, I'm sorry, but I'm worried.'

It was Wilma who saved the day . . . again.

'Mrs Craven,' she said, 'thank you for all the nice things you've said, but seven years ago I was a student. I'm not going in for false modesty. I know I was successful, but the teacher I was with helped me a lot. I wish I could have had even more help than is being suggested now. We worked together. I think we helped the children. I think she found me useful. Recently, I've had students with me – one good, one so-so, but each time they brought an extra pair of hands and both of them brought some new ideas and occasionally new resources, such as reading schemes, from college, which helped me in my teaching. If we are to take more students for longer then that's OK. I won't let them ruin the children's education; I simply won't let them. But if we are to prepare the next generation, we have to do the very best job we can. We must trust them, and I think you must trust us. Don't you see that in your work? On the wards, in the consultation rooms, all the time? Trainees have to learn, people have to be trained. We're a profession – the same as medicine.'

But it was Dr Noble who clinched it.

'I won't waste time revisiting and rehearsing what's already been said. Yes, we must protect the children, we must safeguard their resources *and* we must train the next generation. What occurs to me, though, is that I work in a teaching hospital. We enjoy a higher level of resourcing and attract better qualified staff. I know a lot of positive things have been said today, but underlying the discussion I think I've detected some concern that the school might be damaged by becoming involved in school-based training. I know the analogy with teaching hospitals isn't a true fit, but I believe it could be, maybe even *should* be, and my experience suggests that it will be those schools which do *not* become involved, do *not* become 'training schools' which will in time be seen to have lower status.' She turned to me.

'You have my full support,' she said.

After that, it was time to go home. As I drove away I wondered what lay ahead. In the meeting I'd explained that schools were to be in clusters, with a university tutor attached to each. I hadn't broken the news to them that the Jemima Johnston Primary School was to be in my cluster.

COMMENTARY AND MATTERS FOR DISCUSSION

Partnership between HE and schools

Meetings similar to this one were held everywhere in the country with the arrival of Circular 14/93, which was available in draft form for several months. Nonetheless, universities and colleges have had some difficulty in recruiting sufficient schools to guarantee the thorough school-based nature of their courses. Secondary partnership was probably easier to launch, although arguments about money and funding were fiercer. There was an early realisation that primary partnership offered a different challenge and the 'Brown Book' (DES 1991) had foreshadowed this. Moreover, the relatively equal split between third and fourth year BEd training and PGCE training added a fresh layer of complication. The early assumption that primary partnership would be a 'lesser' thing has not necessarily come about. It is, however, certainly different. Exploring what that difference was began with meetings of this kind and are still being worked out. Craig and Kane (1994) discuss the similarities and differences between primary and secondary partnership ventures.

The catalyst for the move to school-based training was the speech given by the then Secretary of State for Education, Kenneth Clarke, at the North of England Conference – a major annual event – at Southport, 4 January 1992. This coincided with the launch of the 'Brown Book' – *School-based Initial Teacher Training in England and Wales* (DES 1991). The latter was a carefully reasoned report drawing on substantial HMI investigations of a number of school-based pilot studies. Not so temperate was Clarke's speech, which was a series of dramatically presented and colourful proposals aimed primarily at secondary courses of Initial Teacher Training. Clarke wanted schools to be 'in the lead' but, as it transpired, the majority of schools would happily settle for 'partnership'. Schools did not race to seize the opportunity offered by Clarke, and certainly there was much caution about partnership, with primary school partnerships seen to be more problematic than those with secondary schools, due as much as anything to issues of time management and availability of non-contact time. It would be unreasonable and offensive to suggest that primary school teachers have lesser capability than secondary teachers to help prepare new teachers. Mentoring in primary schools evolved not as an inferior version of secondary mentoring, but rather as something quite different, with much turning on the class teacher – an essentially primary school phenomenon. Size of school would however prove to be a factor influencing primary schools' ability to participate. For a discussion of models of partnership with primary schools see Glenny and Hickling (1995), who see the need for an approach which recognises the 'symbiotic relationship that exists between the less and more experienced members of the profession and sets aside the demarcation between INSET and ITT'. Schools acknowledge that the benefits for themselves are not, and are unlikely to be, financial, but there is a growing realisation that there is much quality professional development for teachers, together with opportunities for renewal and refinement of practice. Crowther (1995) and Campbell *et al.* (1998) document how partnership can be developed in ways which enhance teachers' subject knowledge and managerial skills. Crowther cautions schools not just to 'take the money' but to 'open the box' and carefully consider the benefits, issues and problems inside. He also cautions teachers to remember that school-based training initiatives should be set against the background of the attempt to mobilise a 'Mum's Army' to teach Key Stage 1 classes and a squeeze on funding for HE. It is of importance to recall the arguments deployed 20 or so years ago in the battle for an all-graduate profession. Arguably those arguments still apply.

Reform, change or challenge?

For teacher educators, the years following the 1992 speech have been characterised by Bines and Welton (1995: 2) as being of considerable instability, requiring both fast and effective responses.

> Change is interspersed with continuities of concern and intervention in relation to a number of aspects of professional formation and development, ranging from the role and amount of practical teaching experience in initial training to ensuring the right balance between individual and institutional needs in continuing professional development.

Partnership is not uniquely a 1990s phenomenon. Its seeds were sown over several previous years. Schools have always had to work with teacher trainers to arrange school experience placements for students. Various models in the post-war era were typified by the name of the institution – Teacher Training College, College of Education and then Institute of Higher Education or Polytechnic. Bell (1981) suggested that the vision of teacher education offered in each was different, loosely matching the progression of Weber's (1948) three ideal types of educational structure. These moves were from 'charismatic education' to education of the 'cultivated man', to 'specialised expert training'. What vision of education is being presented now? Furlong and Maynard (1995: 11) urge us

> to recognise that throughout the early post-war period none of the changes in teacher education challenged, or were intended to challenge, dominant values or ideologies about school teaching itself.

The debates about the form of teacher training were divorced from the debates about the practice of teaching. Not so in the 1980s and 1990s, where the ideologies of models of training and practices of teaching have become so closely linked, that it could be argued that the new Standards for Qualified Teacher Status (QTS) cover both what to teach and how to teach it.

Other scenarios which demonstrate a conflict of priorities, now becoming all too frequent, are the withdrawal of student places when the brown envelope from OFSTED arrives, or a frantic phone call from a recently retired head teacher's replacement who wants to cancel the school's offer of placements because she was not in post when the deal was made.

Most recently, we have seen school dissatisfaction with the constantly changing regulations and assessment criteria which they find very tiresome and have led some to throw in the towel. An enterprising tutor has counted up the new standards and has come up with 200+ such (see DfEE 1997). Bureaucracy may well have taken over the asylum.

The precarious nature of relationships between schools and universities is all too evident as even more changes and demands are made of teacher education courses, e.g. Circular 14/93 first fully implemented for the September 1996 cohorts, then discarded in 1997, in favour of a National Curriculum for Teacher Training produced around May 1997, which was then overtaken in September 1997 by the new Standards for QTS. What do the majority of schools think of this? Do they have time to read and respond to the endless consultative papers? There must be a sense of *déjà vu*, as they remember the implementation of the National Curriculum. Can schools be expected to be 'in the lead'? Is teacher training one of their priorities? If instead schools settle to be partners with HE, is the partnership 'equal'? Need it be? The Modes of Teacher Education (MOTE)

Project (Furlong *et al.* 1996) found that fully collaborative models were inevitably a small minority of partnerships – almost non-existent, owing to the fact that schools have other matters which take priority over the training of students.

Just who does what is a complex and fraught area. It is not as simple as establishing a theory/practice divide or a division of labour: 'x' in school and 'y' in university. It would appear to be the case that it is the interaction of school and university components, and the professional dialogue between the different partners in a collaboration, which has as much to do with continuing professional development as with initial teacher education, that provides for quality of learning.

Stakeholders in partnerships

Among teacher educators, grappling with the launch of school-based training, the word 'stakeholder' came into common use before it was politically fashionable. It was a helpful word to use to recognise how wide open the field now was. Many different stakeholders are evident in partnership ventures: HE tutors, mentors, class teachers, head teachers, parents and governors being the main ones. The tutors from a university have a major stake in trying to retain what they believe are quality features in their own courses, while striving at the same time to innovate and reconceptualise their roles in the light of government initiatives which have required them to involve teachers in the teaching, supervision and assessment of students. Fish (1995a) discusses these dilemmas and the role of HE tutors and urges HE tutors to 'reclaim their professionalism' by joining with teachers to fight back against government impositions which reduce teachers to 'mere technocrats' and tutors to 'administrators of quality control'. There are inherent tensions in partnerships with schools which come to the fore when negotiations such as those introduced in this tale take place. They are regularly aired at meetings such as this one and then pushed to one side as committed pragmatists take over. However, unless sensitively and carefully handled, they can poison the water in the well of goodwill. A further exploration of how HE tutors see themselves and how they view the reconceptualisation of their role can be found in Campbell and Kane (1996b), in Campbell *et al.* (1998), and in John (1996).

Teachers, in our experience, see themselves primarily and foremost as teachers of children. That they have a valuable contribution to make to the education of student teachers is accepted by all parties involved in partnerships, and much has been written about their role, for example see Fish (1995b), McIntyre, Hagger, and Wilkin (1993), Furlong and Maynard (1995) and McIntyre and Hagger (1996) for further reading. But the pressures experienced by teachers undertaking mentoring are sometimes enough to make them decide to drop out of partnership. The dual roles of teacher of children and tutor to students in the primary school context, unless it is adequately resourced, funded and supported, can result in 'feeling as if you are being pulled in 24 different ways' according to one mentor in a local pilot project. There are often conflicts of interest and difficult decisions to be made when, for instance, a teacher feels that a weak student is hindering the progress of children in her class. Should the student be withdrawn? For the purposes of assessment, there needs to be secure evidence that a student is failing, gained from observation and written reports and the student must have time to amend and adjust teaching after receiving support and advice. So, does 'partnership' imply that the school must now retain the student, and persevere, with all the concomitant problems, as much as anything so that the student can fail 'legitimately'? Not an easy decision! However, arguably the student is now the 'partnership's' student.

Little has been written about either parents' or governors' views about partnership and school-based teacher education, despite the fact that both have potentially much power and influence in primary schools in the 1990s. The *Mentoring in Schools Research Report* (Campbell and Kane 1996b) considered these particular stakeholders and their views, and concluded that parents and governors were interested in school-based training and had some very clear views on it but saw things from a distance. They were normally supportive in principle of students being trained in school and although they expressed concerns, they were realistic ones which had the best interests of the children, the staff, the whole school and not least the students in mind. However, the parents and governors consulted did not see students as a top priority in the school. There were also concerns about whether OFSTED's teaching quality judgements would be affected by student performance and about whether the school would be assessed on how they were training students. Parents were unsure about anything which took the class teacher away from the classroom and could in their view adversely affect their children. Governors felt they ought to be consulted about any new initiatives in school and stressed that the school had limited resources, and that these were to be used for the children. A sense of tentativeness and uncertainty in parents' and governors' responses seems to indicate the precarious, and at times difficult, situations in which schools sometimes find themselves during this decade of intense media and political interest in standards and achievement in education. It is understandable that there may be some reluctance to include parents and governors in discussions, but if schools are to be more involved in teacher education, surely it is of paramount importance to extend the partnership to encompass parents and governors?

FURTHER READING

For an in-depth discussion of the changing political and professional context of teacher education in Britain see the following:

Furlong, J. and Maynard, T. (1995) *Mentoring Student Teachers: The Growth of Professional Knowledge*. London: Routledge. Chapter 1 'Practice makes Perfect?'

Furlong, J. (1992) 'Reconstructing professionalism: ideological struggle in initial teacher education', in Arnot, M. and Barton, L. (eds) *Voicing Concerns: Sociological Perspectives on Contemporary Education Reforms*, Wallingford: Triangle Books.

For a review of partnership see the following:

For a discussion of the MOTE findings see Whiting, C. *et al.* (1996) *Partnership in initial teacher education: a topography*. MOTE Project, Institute of Education, London.

Wilkin, M. (1990) 'The development of partnership in the United Kingdom', in Booth, M., Furlong, J., Wilkin, M. (eds) *Partnership in Initial Teacher Training*. London: Cassell.

Edwards, T. (1995) 'The politics of partnership', in Bines, H. and Welton, J. M. (eds) *Managing Partnership in Teacher Education and Development*. London: Routledge.

Edwards, A. (1996) Endpiece in Edwards, A. and Collison, J. *Mentoring and Developing Practice in Primary Schools*. Milton Keynes: Open University Press.

For a discussion of roles and responsibilities the following references apply:

Campbell, A. and Kane, I. 'The stakeholders: perspectives on school-based training', in Campbell, A. and Kane, I. (1996) *Mentoring in Schools*, the Research Report of the project funded by the Esmée Fairbairn Charitable Trust. (Available from Didsbury School of Education, Manchester Metropolitan University).

Edwards, A. (1996) 'Making the most of relationships with higher education', in Edwards, A. and Collison, J. *Mentoring and Developing Practice in Primary Schools*. Milton Keynes: Open University Press.

CHAPTER 3

Mike's story: failure

Wilma and I had fallen into the habit of extending her MEd tutorial into the pub opposite. The move across the road always signalled, by unspoken agreement, a change in the topic of conversation from the development of her practitioner enquiry – which was about mentoring – to her actual day-to-day experiences in a primary school as a deputy head whose duties included mentoring. The distinction between the two sorts of conversations was subtle but important. Her academic enquiry into aspects of mentoring had been going on for some time and she was a voracious reader. As a result, in my room, we tended to talk about the latest insights she had acquired from the literature. However, during the period of her studies, students had come and gone and she had looked after them. Because she was interested in people generally, she was interested in them as people as much as students and she liked to talk about them. She talked well, but was not beyond a touch of gossip, and from time to time had a dry, disrespectful wit. I enjoyed listening to her. Wilma was by any standards a fine mentor: patient, encouraging, challenging, constructive, supportive – the list of favourable adjectives was extensive. Moreover, as I've explained, she saw students as individuals and was endlessly curious about what made them tick. That night she was in some distress. In the main, Wilma's mentees had been successful. My opinion was that this was not an accident and owed a lot to her. To her other qualities could be added modesty, so that her accounts of the performance of those in her care always tended to attribute success to their talents. That night she needed to talk about Mike, to pour out the problems she knew were there and to address what she saw as her failure. Quite simply, Mike could not do the business.

Mike himself was a lovely guy, keen and enthusiastic, who, in classes and seminars at the university, contributed intelligently and tactfully and generally made the world go round. He is one of those people whom other people like, so much so that students elected him unopposed as their course representative. At the time in question, Mike was on the primary PGCE course. He was a mature entrant, aged 38, and had been an accountant in a textile business. His job security had been looking a bit shaky, but it was not that which had motivated his change of direction. I remember interviewing him. If OFSTED, TTA or indeed anyone wishes to pin the blame for admitting a totally unsuitable student to the course then *mea culpa*, a responsibility, however, which I share with the very experienced headteacher who jointly conducted the interview with me and graded Mike as an 'A' candidate to go with my A/B. My decisiveness is legend. Nonetheless, there had been a small doubt in my mind. There had been a touch of evangelicalism about Mike, a desire to do good openly. Stealth is often the better option. Any doubts I'd had though were banished as he settled into the course and radiated sheer pleasure in his work – joy even. Thinking back, I associate Mike with something Andy Hargreaves and Michael Fullan (1992) wrote in *What's Worth Fighting for in your School?* Their message had had quite an impact upon me: 'Good teaching involves emotional work. It is infused with desire: pleasure, passion, creativity, challenge and joy'. Mike had seemed a natural.

In truth, he had given up his job because he had found it boring. There had been a consequent substantial drop in the family income but he had been sure it would be worth it. Mike is a devout Christian (could this be where the evangelicalism emanated from?). He had become involved with the Scout Movement continuously since his own days in a troop, and he had been a Sunday School teacher almost as long. This two-fold experience with children had been one of the things which had commended him at interview. His move into teaching had had the full support of his wife, and her independently successful career in advertising had enabled them to contemplate the potential loss of income, if not with equanimity, at least with confidence. After all, it would only be for a year, and then Mike would be working again at a lesser, but certainly sufficient, salary with, they both felt sure, good prospects for advancement in Mike's new profession. Many people had assured them that men did well in primary school teaching, especially when they held a good degree in Mathematics from a prestigious university, and when, too, they were a whizz with computers, could surf the Internet, write web pages before breakfast and compile their own CD-Roms for supper. All this, and more, Mike did with his two young primary age children whose early school experiences had contributed to his motivation to teach. How could he lose?

'I cannot escape the suspicion,' said Wilma that night, 'that this guy is a born loser in the classroom. Yet when I look at what he's got going for him, I think it must be me. You give me a silk purse and five weeks into the practice, it's a sow's ear. It must be me.'

I put on my best facilitator voice, 'Would you like to share your problem with me?' I asked.

'I certainly would not,' said Wilma. 'What I'd like to do is tell you what's going wrong and you can tell me how much of it is my fault. If he just isn't going to make it, you can tell me how I tell him and send him back to base with his tail between his legs and his life's ambition in small pieces.'

'That could be a problem,' I said sagely.

'Would you like to share it with me?' said Wilma. I got the message, went off, and bought us each another drink. I prepared to listen.

It transpired that whatever it was that Mike had, it did not include 'presence' in the classroom and no amount of experience of Scout Leadership, Sunday School teaching or family fun had injected into him the necessary charisma. In fact, in the classroom Mike had a personality deficit. He also had a feeble, high-pitched voice which unhappily could be only too easily imitated. In sustained conversation, or during an explanation, his voice additionally became jumpy, ostensibly the product of high nervous energy. Moreover he had drawn too heavily, in his early dealings with the class, upon Scout techniques.

'I didn't mind him getting them all in a circle,' said Wilma, 'although, to be frank, a small classroom and an over-large class of 36 for me made the case fairly strongly for leaving things as they were.'

I smiled thinly.

'No,' said Wilma. 'It was the whistle.'

'He had a whistle?' Slight surprise was in my voice, but then teachers did have whistles . . . always had had whistles. I remembered my own Acme Thunderer which I had proudly bought at the beginning of my first appointment and still kept in a remote drawer with all the other memorabilia of primary school teaching days. 'For the yard games?' I checked.

'For the classroom,' said Wilma glumly. 'Just about every five minutes. It was his control device.'

'It could have worked,' I suggested, tentatively.

'It did work,' said Wilma. 'The first time it worked well, the second time less well, the third time the class were joining in, the next day several had brought their own whistles and by lunchtime the teacher in the class next door was berating me for letting my student get out of control.'

'Don't you mean, it's the class that's out of control?' Wilma had said to her next door neighbour.

'No, I don't,' her colleague had replied, 'and if you don't stop him, I shall personally invade his space, rip his whistle from his mouth and put it . . . well, never mind. Bring him under control!'

'How do you want me to bring him under control?' had been Wilma's enquiry, half-angry, half-beseeching.

'Use a whistle,' said Class Next Door, and stormed off. There was a moment or two's silence.

'I felt such an idiot,' said Wilma.

'I thought you had a behaviour management policy here,' I said. 'Derek's talked about it and I've seen a lot about it in handbooks.'

'We do,' said Wilma, 'and thereby hangs a tale.'

Wilma explained that the school did indeed have a behaviour management policy which, like many schools in that LEA, was based on the principles associated with Assertive Discipline (AD). All staff, including catering, ancillary, administrative and teaching staff had been on training courses over the last few years and were convinced that the school's approach to behaviour management was effective. Parents were aware of the policy, though it often took new pupils' parents some time to understand the system. It was therefore important that staff made every possible effort to help new parents understand the workings of the policy. All this had been explained to Mike. Derek and Wilma had both gone through with him, as they did with all students, some of the key features of the AD approach. These included:

- always praising positive behaviour,
- modification of behaviour through an agreed 5-step procedure of sanctions escalating from having one's name on the board up to five times, reported behaviour, loss of break time, time out of class, and then ultimately time out of school and parental involvement,
- use of certificates, gold stars, and individually negotiated targets and rewards to recognise and reward individual progress,
- use of group incentives and group rewards such as a class marble jar and a variety of small group privileges to recognise and reward group behaviour.

Mike had been enthusiastic. He had taken away the policy along with some further reading. But it all slid away from him. Mike quite simply forgot it in the heat of battle. Unfortunately, he also thought he knew all about class control from the few lectures he'd had on behaviour management and his previous experience of Scout camp leadership. He felt fully equipped with the necessary skills to manage all children, regardless of their background, experience, ability to form relationships with adults and other children, problems of adjustment from a home life very different to school, and their experience of very difficult and abusive situations. All knowledge of these considerations had vanished as the adrenaline spurted with the excitement of oncoming classroom action. On the other hand, as though in another world, he had continued to observe the staff operating the system in the classroom, in the dining room and in the playground. He noted that children who exhibited bad behaviour in the playground were listed by the Lunchtime Organisers (LOs), and when they improved, they were given a little Gold Card as a reward.

'Surely he is into it by now?' I asked.

'Into it!' said Wilma, 'Mike simply cannot leave well alone. He'd make a natural Secretary of State for Education, but he sure is a walking minefield as a teacher. Even after the use and abuse of his whistle, the penny just did not drop.'

It seemed that Mike had thought that it was a pity that the LO seal of approval was not recorded somewhere as mostly these were children who were not widely praised and rewarded for their behaviour and achievement. So he thought. So he decided, off his own bat, to make a chart. He talked to the LO; got access to the LO records and made a rather special chart (fully coloured from his state-of-the-art Apple computer). It showed the children who had received Gold Cards over the term. Obviously it was only those children who had first been identified as having problematic behaviour, so there are only six names on the list. He displayed it in one corner of the classroom, but it transpired that he forgot to tell Wilma about it because she seemed very tied up with the organisation for Parents' Evening.

'The Parents' Evening,' explained Wilma, 'came early on in the school experience, before I had really sussed out that Mike was a failing student. I fixed him up to attend as part of his school experience, and in order to tick it off on his wretched competences list. It was an opportunity to help him develop "the ability to report to parents", so I invited him and suggested that he chatted informally to parents after my more formal session, and that he introduced them to the displays around the room.'

Wilma explained the variety of displays. There was 'Music from around the World', 'Divali', 'Artists from Holland', 'Equivalent Fractions' and more.

'But,' and she closed her eyes and clenched her teeth, 'there were also various organisational/print in the environment/notices/records/announcement/type of displays.'

I nodded. 'Of course.'

'In my class,' continued Wilma 'was one Cheryl Summers, a new child in the class, coming from another very different school in the very affluent suburbs of the city. Her mother had already come across to me as concerned that her daughter should get the best chance in life. I have to tell you, she has a bit of a down on teachers, having failed to get on the local uni BEd course, so thank you for that. She had already made herself known to most of the staff, and certainly to the Head, as one to handle carefully. She was being taken round the classroom displays by Mike in 'my name is Mike and I'll be your host tonight' style, when he came to the chart. She asked why her Cheryl's name was not on the Gold Card list and Mike told her that at Jemima Johnston only the naughty children are eligible for Gold Cards. Now to Mrs Summers a Gold Card is a sacred object, and I've wondered myself whether it was the wisest choice as a record of crime expiation but to her, well, she went ballistic, rushed out of the classroom straight to the Head's room, shouting about "equal opportunities" and "damn silly" discipline systems which meant that well-behaved children like her daughter couldn't be praised and rewarded, couldn't have a Gold Card, and how she was going to speak to her councillor, her MP, the press and so on and so on.'

'Did she?'

'Yes, and the correspondence is still going on. I suppose it wasn't all his fault, but he is uniquely capable of upsetting all creatures great and small. It's not just parents. You should see him with hamsters.'

Wilma stayed silent for a moment or two. Then she shuddered and warmed to her theme.

'Very early on he decided he was going to do a natural history lesson about hamsters. He went to a lot of trouble to arrange to borrow a hamster from the pet shop in the Market Square. He had such plans for drawings and stories. He had worksheets galore. It was a beautiful day. All the conditions for success were present. He'd built the class up the day before about the surprise visitor. Cometh the hour. In he marched after the Assembly, bearing a large veterinary box, containing – as I knew but the class didn't – one small hamster.

"Open the windows", he said, "and let's breathe in the lovely fresh air." They did. "And now," he said, like Marvo the Magician, "here is our big surprise visitor," and he lifted the lid and reached in. Alas, Hammy the Heroic Hamster was too quick for him. Up, up and away, out of the box, over the desks, on to the pipes, up to the window. Gone. The lesson had been going thirty seconds and its sole focus had vanished in a flash. What were we to do for the remaining 59 minutes and 30 seconds?'

'I can't imagine. Tell me.'

'I was inspired, simply inspired. Now I knew what mentoring really was. "Oh dear," I said, "oh dear, oh dear. Mr Shelton why don't you take the class out on to the field, it's a lovely day, and look for Hammy? Meanwhile, I'll get in touch with the AA." He looked at me like as I was demented but he was too banjaxed by Hammy's disappearing act to object and he promptly marched them on to the field. I, for my part, shot out to my car and raced three miles to the Square for a hamster replacement kit, and got back just in time. Mike was wandering the field despairingly and the kids were rampaging here, there and everywhere.

"I've found Hammy," I shouted. "Why don't you bring the class back in?" He looked so relieved, my heart melted. "Here," I said, "you'll need this" and I handed him his whistle, but I made sure I got it back when they were all safely returned.'

There was more to come as Wilma explained how the computer wizard dream had turned into a nightmare, how Mike had frequently become obsessed with what a trio of children were doing on the computer, had got pulled into their work and within no time at all he was doing it not only with them but for them. Meanwhile 33 other children had quickly gone off task finding a variety of substitutes for the carefully prepared worksheets which Mike had devised, produced, written and printed off.

'I talked to him and talked to him and talked to him,' agonised Wilma. 'I explained and explained and he nodded and agreed and said he had registered the point and promised to address it in the next lesson and it would all be OK and he did and it was, for a while, but then he wandered off to the computer workstation and once again there was chaos. So I fixed it.'

'What did you do?' I was genuinely curious.

'I took the computer off him.'

'As well as the whistle?'

'Well sort of,' said Wilma.

In practice she had taken him aside afterwards and attributing some of the blame to herself, she had persuaded him that they – she and Mike – had planned too wide a variety of activity in the classroom, which had led to too much movement, making for problems of order and control, but more particularly spreading Mike too thinly. Four groups were plenty they had agreed, which had tended in the event to work out as three for her and one for Mike.

'Did he have any comments to offer?'

'Oh, yes,' said Wilma. 'He had been shocked to find that there was only one computer. He thinks every child should have his or her own.'

'He's right,' I said helpfully.

'Thank you,' said Wilma, 'I'll mention it to the Head when next I see him.'

The odd thing was that despite Mike's face-to-face encounter with resource issues, he was an exuberant enthusiast for state education. His own experiences as a boarder at a well-known public school had left him with very sad memories of a lonely, loveless, highly competitive but privileged schooling. He had been put off the private system and this had led him to argue powerfully and successfully with Emma, his wife, about their own children's education. As a result their two children both attended the only primary school in the local village. As far as I could tell from talking to him, he was every teacher's dream as a parent helper – a quiet, unobtrusive, courteous, computer specialist, with an engaging habit of bringing in little extras for the classroom hardware. In many ways he had helped the local school some way along the road to the wealth of computers which he saw as every child's classroom entitlement. There remained, alas, the problem that the schools in Mike's personal experience were a far cry from those he had been visiting or been attached to on his PGCE course and very different indeed from the Jemima Johnston Primary School. This had given Wilma another problem.

'I know all about the statutory requirements accompanying the National Curriculum; I go along – not without difficulty – with the collective worship requirement, and I'm as broadly Christian as the next person, but this is a school with a number of ethnic minorities represented and such windows of opportunity as do exist for multi-faith religious education should be opened. Mike steams up the windows.'

I didn't know about Wilma's being 'as broadly Christian as the next person.' At that moment I was the next person and I wasn't sure how I measured up; certainly by comparison with Wilma, who was in practice the school's RE co-ordinator, which is why I was interested in what Wilma meant about steaming up the windows.

'He hasn't got many RE lessons,' said Wilma, 'and he has a self-confessed weakness in the area of multi-faith education, so we have talked about this at some length and I fully expected . . . well I'm not quite sure what I fully expected, but what I didn't expect was three lessons which ended up dedicated to, "that" commandment, you know, well sort of, "Thou Shalt Not Come Into Dudley".'

'Dedicated to what?' I queried sharply.

'You know,' said Wilma, 'what the kids always say, like Gladly the Cross-Eyed Bear and A Maiden's Grave when they mean Gladly the Cross I'd Bear or Amazing Grace. So . . . Thou Shalt Not Come Into Dudley.'

'The commandment?'

'Well one of them.'

I was still looking puzzled. Wilma spelt it out for me: 'Commit adultery. Come into Dudley. Yes?'

'He taught three lessons on the Ten Commandments?' I gulped.

'Certainly did, but in the end it boiled down to just one.'

'Dudley?'

'Dudley.'

'Tell me more,' I groaned.

After extensive discussion with Wilma, it had been agreed that Mike would design and teach a session – more moral education than RE – about 'Rules which help us live together'. He had chosen to get there by opening up on the Ten Commandments. When he had originally discussed it all with Wilma the intention had been the other way round, to work towards the Ten Commandments. Mike had turned the agreed planning process on its head. He had produced a worksheet on which ten clouds floated serenely. In each cloud was written a commandment. Then Mike had taken one of the commandments – he had chosen gluttony – and illustrated, quite cleverly, how one might keep the commandment, and how one might break it. He had then supplied a further sheet, with a blank cloud and a blank box. The class had been invited to illustrate, as Mike had done, how one might keep their chosen commandment and – at this point, Wilma's face was a picture – also how one might break it.

By and large, the children at Jemima Johnston are streetwise, and had had good sex education. The children in that particular Year 6 class were quite precocious. They were interested in sex in a Year 6 sort of way, but more than anything they were interested in having a good laugh at the expense of teachers and students. I could see only too clearly where Wilma was going with her story.

'I don't suppose he got many pictures of his neighbour's ox?' I ventured.

'Nul points.'

'Dudley?'

'Dudley.'

'I'm not sure,' I ventured, 'that I wouldn't put that down to naivety and inexperience.'

Wilma was forthright: '*I'm* not naive,' she said, 'and *I'm* not inexperienced, and I'd told him to be careful, and I'd warned him about the Ten Commandments, but he'd said he'd done it all before in Sunday School and it had worked really well and he wanted to try it. So we worked out the best way to do it, then he goes and turns it all over, comes at it in totally the wrong way, and there's chaos . . . and parents complaining. He says he's very sorry and he sees that he might have been a little ambitious. Class Next Door says he's a raving idiot and that it's my fault, states again that I'm the mentor and asks why can't I control him. So, he goes out and buys her flowers, apologises for the trouble and noise and hopes that he can learn from his mistakes. She's charmed. I don't get flowers. He doesn't minister in any way to my bruised feelings, so meanwhile, I wonder just how bad I can get as a mentor.'

'What *can* he do?' I asked.

'He can do Maths,' said Wilma, 'but he can't teach it, and he's got a Maths degree, for goodness sake. But he's so good at Maths that he can't begin to comprehend life in the slow lane. He did decimal fractions with Yellow group. Whatever it is that is going on, and required in the National Curriculum, I can assure you that Yellow group are "working towards" it. This blew his mind. It was the same as with the computer workstation. Once he'd realised that here was a group of children who lacked an immediate understanding of the topic and, quite frankly, couldn't do anything on his worksheet, he went like a bee to a honey pot. Zooming in on that group with that problem, he neglected everything else, and what might be going wrong in other groups and left them to their own devices.'

I was curious. 'What did they do?'

'The wicked ones did evil things with dangerous and sharp mathematical instruments which he had left on his desk, open at the place. The quiet ones drew clouds with matching illustrations. After that it was Humanities. We're doing a project on Australia. Do you know what he said to me before today's lesson started? He said that he wasn't getting much comeback on his boomerang topic. So he decided to revert to Scouthood – Cubs actually, and he talked to them about Mowgli and the Jungle Book. He put up some pictures of lions and tigers.'

'I didn't know there were lions and tigers in Australia,' I said.

'Tell me about it.'

'You make it sound a lot of fun,' I persevered.

'It's not.' Wilma shook her head. 'That was this morning. By lunchtime he was in tears. Fortunately it was games in the afternoon and we were both free. Then, and subsequently, all we've done is talk about it. I'm not sure I can take a nice man of 38 in tears because his dream is shattered, his life plan laid waste and his family income severely damaged. And I can't help thinking that it's my fault.'

There was a double problem here. I rated Wilma very highly as I have explained before, and of course I knew her as a student. Mentoring was something she was very interested in. I didn't want that interest destroyed. Moreover, I trusted her judgement, which meant that, if half of what she said was true, then Mike was not for teaching. He should be made to recognise this at that stage and the issue of his unsuitability for teaching should not be allowed to drag on. Meanwhile I had to make Wilma recognise that some students will never make teachers. The fault is no more that of the mentor to whom they are attached than it is that of the university which admitted them in the first place. Almost certainly less. Wilma was not responsible for Mike's career change choice. She was totally removed from his family circumstances; she had no control over his funny voice, his nervous manner or his feeble classroom personality. She had prepared him thoroughly for the lessons and she had identified danger zones. She had correctly indicated things which probably would work and things which probably wouldn't. He was clearly a nice guy – but odd. Unfortunately, he was equally clearly a natural target for cruel classroom humour. He did not command respect and I had been unable to identify in anything Wilma had told me any sign of real affection between the children and Mike. Wilma lacked only one thing – the experience of telling a student that, come what may, in her opinion, he or she was not going to make it. The first time is always the hardest. It gets easier, because underneath the real-life cases is the fundamental priority, the welfare of children. Schools do not need poor teachers. Sometimes it is necessary to convey this difficult truth. I was certain that as she gained in experience Wilma would absorb all this. She would see the failure, but ultimately she would come to understand and recognise that the failure was not hers. On this occasion she would need some support.

I decided that this was a role for the university tutor, Jeremy, who had shared the supervision with Wilma. I wondered slightly why she hadn't mentioned him. It would appear that this was another facet of Wilma's obsessive perception of Mike's case as 'her' failure and her manifest reluctance to expose her thinking to the tutor in question. I tracked him down to his room the following day. He delivered his verdict. There had been some problems in the classroom, but nothing that couldn't be put right. Mike was very good under questioning from Jeremy, about his work.

'Every time I've seen him, the lesson has been generally acceptable.'

'Which was . . . ?' I pressed.

'Twice.'

It was clear that my colleague, Jeremy, was extremely impressed by Mike's degree and his mathematical ability.

'It's this sort of quality which we need in the profession.'

Most of all he was impressed by Mike's meticulous file and his ability to analyse the classroom and school context. However, my colleague was not without worry. He expressed a concern about how Mike was coping with 'a very challenging school and a very challenging staff'.

'The mentor rarely leaves him alone, you know. She's at him all the time. She's very critical and I think she's undermining his confidence. She's got a lot to learn about supporting weak students. Frankly, Mike's confessed to me that she frightens him. He much prefers the teacher in the class next door.'

COMMENTARY AND MATTERS FOR DISCUSSION

Failing your students

Wilma felt she was a failure. It is quite common, for mentors, certainly as they discharge the role for the first few times, and even subsequently, to feel that if their student has failed then they too have somehow failed as a mentor. Teachers find the assessment part of mentoring to be difficult. Partnership has sharpened the focus. Close daily contact, regular support, ongoing, formative assessment aimed at helping students to amend their teaching, and the forging of close working relationships can make the assessment process in partnership schemes problematic. Mentors are particularly subject to pressure at the summative stage, with the majority having the wholly understandable desire to pass students rather than fail them. Edwards and Collison (1996) identify the mentor's dilemma of being 'teacherly friend and final arbiter' and recognise the 'sense of personal failure when students they have personally nurtured still fail to reach appropriate standards'. Fish (1995a) acknowledges the complexity and problematic nature of assessing student teachers and stresses the need for skilled observation in order to improve the quality of feedback to students. Devlin (1995) describes how assessment can be a 'burden to mentors who felt ill-equipped without higher education support' to discuss fully the strengths and weaknesses of students, bringing a central issue to the fore, that of collaboration between university and school in the assessment process. Observation and assessment of students is a key element of mentor preparation and training, and arguably ought to be the focus for collaborative work with tutors in universities to enable joint assessment of students.

Competence-based assessment

How would Mike fare, measured on the new scale and in the new language of competences? Was his performance on parents' evening that of a potentially competent beginning teacher? Were all his other disasters no more than the inevitable errors of the tyro? Or were there more fundamental faults? Discussion about assessment is these days frequently linked to competences, and not even their recent conversion to standards causes the issues to disappear. Circular 14/93 brought competences to the centre of all teacher-trainers' consciousness in primary teacher education a year or so behind secondary education. Critiques of these frameworks of competences consistently identify the dangers of the crude nature of the concepts of competence presented and the restricted notions of professionality which ignore the problematic nature of teaching. Pring (1995: 199) summarises the arguments

> Governments whether to the Right or the Left who seek to control outcomes – to bureaucratise education and turn it into something else, to transform teachers into deliverers of a curriculum – will no doubt be seduced by this temptation. They will ignore the complexities of these notions and treat them as though they can be reduced to simple definitions.

Worries about distortion of what teachers actually do are compounded by the lack of practitioner involvement in these externally imposed requirements. Whitty and Willmott (1995), however, are not so concerned. They propose that competence-based approaches may have a number of benefits, such as demystifying teacher education; identifying a clearer role for schools and HE in the training process; greater confidence on the part of employers as to what beginning teachers can do, and clearer goals for students. They also identify the difficulties which include reductionism, specification and determining valid and reliable criteria for assessment. Caution as to the dangers of a narrowly mechanistic approach to assessing initial teacher education abound in the literature as do calls to remember that teaching is both multifaceted and culture-dependent (Furlong 1995). McIntyre and Hustler (1996) in their concluding comments remind us that assessment is both formative and summative and identify tensions which cause problems when attempting to profile personal qualities, so important to the beginning teacher, as demonstrated in most of the tales in this book. One contemporary challenge for the late 1990s for teacher educators is how to match the competences of Circular 14/93 to the standards in Circular 10/97. The OFSTED/TTA *Framework for the Assessment of Quality and Standards* (1996) has needed to be rapidly revised. HMI, in conference, managed to turn competences into standards quite quickly. Some parts of the system report more difficulty. Will we be able to see the joins? And how does becoming a reflective practitioner fit in? Sutherland (1997) endorses the concept. Mike was competent in his IT knowledge and skills but lacked the ability to transform knowledge and skills into appropriate and relevant classroom activities for primary pupils. Could it be reasonably expected that he would slowly, even painfully, learn to make the transformation or was he the classic 'hopeless case'?

Characteristics of failure

Was Mike failing? The characteristics of failing students are diverse and complex and are largely under-researched, but Maynard (1997), in her helpful guidance to mentors involved in assessing students, unsurprisingly concludes *inter alia*, 'Often the effectiveness of the student's classroom control is considered inadequate' and few would dissent from the view that a class out of control is a sign of failure. However, she also identifies lack of appreciation of the demands of being a professional educator as another area. Who could deny that Mike was being blown away on both these counts? However, by far the most difficult students to deal with, in her opinion, are 'those who display certain personality characteristics which make them unsuitable for entry into the teaching profession'. Did not Mike fall into this category? 'Presence' in the classroom and appropriate behaviour are so dependent on how a teacher or student teacher projects his or her personality and asserts authority, that failure to do so usually results in failure on the course. All that said, Mike's tutor, Jeremy, did not see him at all as a failing student. It is at this point that most partnerships throw the ball to a further arbiter. If it is an assessed practice, an external examiner becomes the *deus ex machina*. It is surely appropriate nowadays for mentors and tutors to be able to make up their collective minds – and take a decision.

Stages and levels of development in students

Was Mike being suitably trained, mentored and inducted? Learning to teach is a complex and challenging activity which is the subject of substantial, international investigation and research. Edwards and Collison (1996: 20–23) in their discussion of students as learners offer a Vygotskian framework for a training partnership. Implicit is the need for clearly defined experiences for students which may not always involve teaching. They cite observation and guided discussion as two valuable other elements. This Vygotskian model moves students cyclically through four quadrants consisting of:

(a) an introduction to key ideas in educational theory as they relate to classroom practice;
(b) making sense of what they have heard, read and seen in university and school so that 'knowledge about teaching' from university can be brought nearer to the 'knowledge of how to teach' from school;
(c) students being placed in 'safe' and well constructed classroom contexts to work out their ideas about teaching children;
(d) a concluding phase, when students are more confident, and they demonstrate their understanding by putting their knowledge into action.

Mike had, it would appear, got stuck somewhere between stages (b) and (c). Mentors and tutors are of key importance in each of these stages, though their roles would vary depending on the stage of the student. Edwards and Collison acknowledge that one of the difficulties of school-based training is that because of their impatience to be teachers, students are all too ready to present themselves immediately as competent teachers and tend to see quadrants (c) and (d) as the same stage. This may well link with the lack of challenge identified in Chapter 6, 'Triumph and disaster', therefore making more difficult the mentor's task of stimulating the student to aid development of teaching. Edwards and Collison rightly identify quadrant (c) as the crucial area for mentoring, where 'simply trying out ideas is not enough'. They argue that students need a mentor who is a 'conversationalist and guide'. The importance of the notion of a 'community of practice' as developed by Lave and Wenger (1991) is relevant: all those taking part in the community locate and develop knowledge in the field in order to induct novices into the profession. The community can be a school, but a wider interpretation of community is applicable when talking about partnership ventures and school-based teacher education, and would include a university. In such 'communities of practice' students need to become 'legitimate peripheral participants'. The Lave and Wenger argument is that students cannot learn if they are full participants so they therefore need to negotiate a further role separate from teaching; one which allows them to be a learner and observer.

Maynard and Furlong (1993) developed an analysis of student progress which had five stages:

(a) early idealism – tending to identify more with pupils than teachers;
(b) survival – becoming obsessed with classroom control and 'fitting in';
(c) recognising difficulties – becoming sensitive to the varied demands made on them and worrying about whether they would pass, focusing on methods and resources;
(d) 'hitting the plateau' – finding a way to teach and sticking to it but finding difficulty in shifting the focus from themselves to others and 'connecting these activities to what pupils should be learning over time' (Feiman-Nemser and Buchmann 1987);
(e) moving on – going on to experiment and be concerned for pupils' learning.

Maynard and Furlong stress the need for intervention, if students' level of reflection is to rise above being shallow and ineffective.

Craft knowledge

Whichever of the above constructions one examines, Mike barely progressed beyond the earliest stages.

Where do you start? What elements of the teacher's role can you leave until a later date before they are brought into focus? The nature of the job is that all elements of the role are on view and working in a complex and highly interdependent system. It is difficult to be selective and thus not overload the student at the start.

These are the words of a mentor quoted in Campbell and Kane (1996b: 86).

The above discussion of stages and levels highlights again the importance of active mentoring and of students being willing to engage in a dynamic process of critical analysis which involves direct, concrete talk about teaching and the ability to take on board constructive feedback. Mike was unable to take on board his mentor's constructive feedback. Wilma did try to give him access to her 'craft knowledge' but he lacked understanding of teaching and learning. There are issues relating specifically to 'craft knowledge'. McIntyre and Hagger (1993) have expressed reservations about students' ease of access to such knowledge. The assumptions expressed by Boydell (1994) that 'mentoring within a wider cluster of schools will almost certainly be a powerful influence on students' professional development' are as yet relatively unexplored in mentoring partnerships, although the work of Edwards and Collison (1996) goes a long way to opening up the possibilities. Edwards and Collison drew attention to the difficulties faced by experienced teachers in making their 'tacit professional knowledge explicit and readily available in ways that a novice can grasp or even recognise'. The issue of how to communicate 'craft knowledge' is also acknowledged by teachers themselves, in Campbell and Kane (1996a). The assumptions that 'classroom experience automatically provides the most appropriate learning' or that 'more experience is better experience,' may yet prove to be incorrect as heralded by Dunne and Harvard (1993). There is, in any case, an underlying problem in describing and making explicit, craft knowledge. Much discussion between mentors and students still draws heavily on as yet unsystemised, uncategorised, prior practice.

Subject knowledge

Whatever his deficiencies, Mike was a high quality graduate, with a good degree in a core subject, and considerable expertise in IT.

Criticisms of both students' and teachers' lack of appropriate subject knowledge abound in recent reports (OFSTED 1993, TTA 1995) and in the media at large. But are the powers that pronounce clear about what subject knowledge is and what its relationship to pedagogical subject knowledge might be? Shulman (1986) proposes that an amalgam of general pedagogical knowledge (non-specific, classroom management and pupil discipline) and subject knowledge (knowledge as it might be known to a graduate, prior to any attempt to teach it) forms the essence of what teachers need to know. This goes beyond personal subject knowledge. At the heart of pedagogical subject knowledge is the 'transformation' of subject knowledge. This is what Mike could not achieve, able and knowledgeable man that he was. According to Shulman (1986), the following four sub-processes could be argued for as necessary conditions for 'transformation':

1. critical interpretation of the relevant content in planning what to teach;
2. representation via a repertoire of analogies, activities and alternative ways of explanation in order to make the subject more understandable;
3. adaptation – implying knowledge of the learner's preconceptions or possible misconceptions;
4. tailoring – referring adaptations to particular pupils.

The term 'transformation' is useful as it implies that the teaching process involves more than the straightforward 'application' or 'delivery' of teachers' subject knowledge. Another interesting concept, which helps explore issues concerning subject knowledge is that of 'school knowledge', Banks *et al.* (1996), by which is meant subject knowledge as transposed into specifically school curricula, as in texts, school or departmental curriculum policies, prescriptions and interpretations of the National Curriculum.

The knowledge base for teaching has become a contentious area and is also a focus for research, several projects asserting that increasing a teacher's subject knowledge has in the event little correlation with an ability to teach a subject effectively, Ferguson and Womack (1993) and Harlen (1996). If 'subject matter is only half the story' as Edwards and Collison (1996) report, then the other half involves the conversion of that subject matter into learning activities. The conversion involves two processes. Initially, 'depersonalised and decontextualised' public discourse of the subject must be transferred into an environment which motivates and connects with the learner. Then, secondly, the process of enabling the learner to function in the subject discipline discourse must occur, Meredith (1995). Part of the task is to assess what is appropriate for primary age learners in terms of subject knowledge. This is a not insubstantial challenge for the future! Meanwhile we live with the Noddy definition of subject knowledge supplied in Circular 10/97, viz.:

2. Primary

For all courses, those to be awarded Qualified Teacher Status, must, when assessed, demonstrate that they:

f. for any specialist subject(s), have a secure knowledge of the subject to at least a standard approximating to GCE Advanced level in those aspects of the subject taught at KS1 and KS2.

Powerful stuff!

FURTHER READING

A useful unit on assessment and mentoring can be found in Kerry, T. and Shelton Mayes, A. (1995) *Issues in Mentoring*. London: Routledge. In this unit there are chapters by Richard Pring, on standards and quality in education; Geoff Whitty, on quality control in teacher education; Geoff Whitty and Elizabeth Willmott, on competence-based teacher education: approaches and issues; John Furlong, the limits of competence: a cautionary note; Bob Moon and Ann Shelton Mayes, integrating values into the assessment of teachers in initial education and training.

For a comprehensive look at competence-based teacher education initiatives see Hustler, D. and McIntyre, D. (eds) (1996) *Developing Competent Teachers: Approaches to Professional Competence in Teacher Education*. London: David Fulton Publishers. There is a case study from Manchester: Hogbin, J., Cockett, P., Hustler, D. 'Diversity, change and continuity: developing institutional policy at the Manchester Metropolitan University'. This may also provide added contextual information about the courses in which our fictional student characters were located. It might even explain some of their idiosyncracies.

Della Fish (1995a) in *Quality Mentoring for Student Teachers: A Principled Approach*, London: David Fulton Publishers, provides, in Chapter 7, a good discussion and a set of issues for group work on matters concerning competence and assessment.

For a fuller explanation and application of Furlong and Maynard's (1993) stages of student development see Chapter 5 in Furlong, J. and Maynard, T. (1995) *Mentoring Student Teachers: the Growth of Professional Knowledge*. London: Routledge. Chapter 2 may also be of interest: Learning to Teach – the competency-based model.

Those wishing to pursue the 'communities of practice' notion will find Lave, J. and Wenger, E. (1991) *Situated Learning: Legitimate Peripheral Participation*, Cambridge: Cambridge University Press, a worthwhile read.

Further exploration of subject knowledge issues can be found in:

Bennett, N. and Carre, C. (Eds) (1993) *Learning to Teach*. London: Routledge.
Maynard, T. (1996) 'Mentoring subject knowledge in the primary school', in McIntyre, D. and Hagger, H. *Mentors in Schools: Developing the Profession of Teaching*. London: David Fulton Publishers.

CHAPTER 4

Sharon's story: success

I was walking the corridors, humming to keep my spirits up, having just plucked from my pigeonhole the somewhat apologetic memo from on high, notifying the primary team that we were about to be inspected for the third consecutive year. I knew this meant work for me. The memo had stressed that the emphasis of that year's inspection would be on the way mentors in schools were being prepared to train students to teach personal, social and moral education, physical education and aspects of what used to be called Home Economics. Thank goodness, they hadn't been around for Mike and the Commandments. None of these is my personal area of expertise, so I would not be going under the subject surgeon's knife. I am, however, very much involved in all aspects of mentor preparation and training. It would be wrong to say that I had initiated, personally, a great deal of the training which bore upon moral and physical well-being. Offhand I was struggling to think of anything, although we had done a fair bit of work on how these issues arise in the context of mentoring students. I was feeling somewhere between numb and resilient. I had become, like so many of my colleagues, inspection-happy, pretty much braindead, so what was one more? In this way I was talking myself into 'rough, tough mouse' mode and consoling myself that things could not get much worse, when they did. Trish – a colleague at that time supervising students at Jemima Johnston – popped out of her room.

'Oh, there you are,' she said, 'I was looking for you.' (She often is.) 'Boy, do *we* have a problem!'

'We?' I asked. 'Who's this "we"?'

'Well, not really "we",' she said, 'more "you". There's a bit of a crisis at J J.'

I looked at her, quickly remembering what it was about her that put her medium to low down on my list of favourite tutors. Basically she was a 'dumper'. Problem-solving was not her strength. She had strengths, but her capacities stopped well short of crisis management. She did have a line, from time to time, in crisis precipitation or crisis development but unfailingly it was when the crisis was nicely cooking and beyond the point where sensible action would have arrested it, that she brought it to the appropriate person and delegated it upwards. I did not yet have any details but I had a hunch that the problem was going to be, according to her, 'the student'. This was not because there was anything wrong with either of the students she was supervising.

Indeed, I rated them both highly. Rather it was that Trish had some problems with the generation gap.

She had come into teacher training a year previously, in her early forties, having been on a three-year attachment to the LEA from her school, where she had been a deputy head, and an advisory teacher responsible for assessment in the primary curriculum. She had entered her new role with us full of enthusiasm but with very high expectations of the students. Sometimes she also revealed over-high expectations of teachers themselves. She found it hard to work with 'average' people. She was quite unused to working with younger members of the teaching profession, mostly having worked with heads, deputies and more experienced teachers. This particular supervision was only the second time that she had done any solo flying. I knew her to be conscientious, thorough, and good at dealing with senior folk in the school. She would have been punctual in visiting, punctilious in her protocols and would have loads of notes and would also have left extensive comments in the students' files. She would have given them her home phone number, conscientiously followed up any issues, and begun to construct her own mental profile of their strengths and weaknesses. The students would not be regarding her with any great affection, but she would have their respect. Add to this rosy scenario the fact that both students were well-above average, indeed very strong, and that both mentors were experienced and enthusiastic. I had not expected trouble. I suspected something nasty had fallen down the generation gap. I was half right in the event.

'Which student?' I came straight to the point.

'Sharon.'

Now I was really perplexed. I have said that both students were strong, but I knew Sharon to be exceptionally good. Moreover, her mentor was Meg, a really top-of-the-range mentor. This was a partnership made in heaven. Sharon had come to us with three A levels, (all As). Her main subject was English and she was doing extremely well on the course – on track for top grades in everything. She had shown herself to be a pleasant, assertive, energetic young woman of twenty-two, albeit somewhat frenetic and hyper. She was articulate and friendly with a sharp witty manner. Her speciality was devising activities which captured children's imaginations and kept them interested for substantial periods of time. She worked at a classroom pace of 100 miles an hour, was full of great ideas and wanted to try them all out. To be fair, she had a bit of a reputation with her peers as Little Miss Perfect, owing to the fact that she always liked to be best at everything. Her attention to detail was meticulous, and she would go through her tutor's and mentor's comments with a fine tooth comb, and answer every question raised – in coloured biro, while providing supporting details to elaborate her points of view. But she was more than a classroom-bound visionary. She was enthusiastic in joining in amateur drama productions which contributed no doubt to her vibrant and enthusiastic presence in the classroom and school. So, Sharon was an able student, but one who often made others less gifted only too aware of their weaknesses by her exuberant approach to teaching and school life. I wondered if she was beginning to have that effect on Meg. I doubted it. Meg was a powerful personality.

I could go on about Sharon. As the only child of devoted parents, she had had every opportunity they could afford – travel, world trips, India, Pakistan, China, South America – which had afforded her the opportunity to gain first-hand knowledge of many of the countries from which several of the Jemima Johnston children originated. Her artistic skills – yes, those as well – enabled her to construct excellent displays and exciting classroom interactive areas. Sharon liked to be challenged – unfortunately her previous school experiences had been low on challenge. A problem was that she fitted so well into the context, quickly developed her teaching and was encouraged to get on with it. Her previous teachers and tutors frequently asked 'How can you improve such an able student?' Some felt redundant, others let her get on with it. Yet, there were some areas where Sharon needed challenge and support – such as assessing and recording children's achievement in oracy and drama; meeting special educational needs of a diverse group of second language learners; developing strategies for promoting children's independence and responsibility. It was for this reason mainly that I had assigned Trish to her.

'Let them drive each other demented,' I had thought constructively.

I did have one or two worries about her, particularly about her intensity. By contrast with other students she seemed both young and old for her age. I had no hard and fast knowledge, just a few bits of what I'd heard, what others had said and indeed odd remarks she had made herself. It appeared to me that Sharon had missed out on some aspects of life, mainly those related to a social life. She never had a steady boyfriend as far as I could tell and many of her peer group at college seemed too immature or wimpy for her liking. Accordingly, she spent much of her time working in the library, even those times when it would be normal to be in the bar, or gossiping in the common room. I knew that she had been to a convent school for girls in a rural setting, with very limited opportunities for meeting young men, even immature and wimpy ones. She had led a rather sheltered life, I guessed. Such experience as she'd had had been limited. I wondered if she had been putting herself under too much pressure that she'd blown a fuse. Maybe some of her weaknesses had surfaced. In theory, she knew a lot, but maybe it had gone wrong. It was still very surprising because I felt sure she would be receiving excellent support from her mentor, Meg.

Meg was in her thirties, and Head of the Early Years, KS1 department. She was a lively, articulate, bright, resourceful teacher. Sometimes she'd ventured the view that the rest of the staff were often a bit staid and slow to try out new ideas. Her classroom environment was stimulating, constantly changing and never dull. She had mentored five or so students before and been very successful in that they had all gained high grades. She was a challenging mentor who also gave high levels of support. She worked with both pupils and students at a rigorous pace, had high expectations, but, at the same time, was sensitive to the need for all to achieve. She was perceptive in her interpersonal relationships, was a good facilitator, had trained as a counsellor for Relate on marriage guidance work and her interpersonal skills were often employed to resolve staff and pupil conflict.

This particular placement was nearing its end. By coincidence I'd been chatting to Derek, the Head, at a local LEA meeting about four or five weeks earlier. My mind flashed back to that conversation and my puzzlement increased. I began to recall his comments.

'Meg's had such a wonderful time mentoring Sharon. She's done such a good job.' He dived into his case and pulled out a thick file. 'Look,' he said, 'I've actually got her mentor's log here. It's fascinating reading.'

Although I'd already got the message, he read me some of the comments:

February 17

Worked with S this afternoon on devising a structured play area to promote children's thinking skills. Not an area that I've tackled before. Found S had really thought it through, had done lots of research and brought in the Edward De Bono materials and some more challenging, thought-provoking articles by Fuerstein, an Israeli psychologist who has been working in this area. Must follow this up in my local library . . . Realise that despite my ignorance in this area I have unconsciously been developing children's thinking through my problem-solving corner. S was impressed by the range of activities and suggested that she and I could collate them for a handbook for rest of staff and maybe her tutor would be interested in circulating it to students.

What have I learned this week?

- the need to get better at explaining why I do certain things
- the need for concrete precise talk about teaching when team planning
- some gaps in my observation techniques (need to go on course)
- the importance of research when devising new activities and curriculum plans.

'I have to say,' he continued, 'the benefits of having such a good student and such an able mentor have been terrific for the school.'

I was interested in what he was saying, as he moved on to exemplify the professional benefits for teachers of being involved in mentoring.

'Meg's been on five short courses this term, Maths, English, Technology, Geography and Ceramics – her classroom is full of junk models, homemade triangular prisms, plans, maps and weather vanes, and now she is interested in having a kiln. That's where Sharon's been a godsend. She's doing all the research on cost and practicality and your Trish is good too. Now, *there's* someone who really knows her stuff about assessment. Once I knew what she'd been doing before you took her out of useful service, and whom she'd been working with, I signed her up. She's done three INSET sessions for the staff, and the impact on the school has been great.'

What I've just described was part of my drowning-person syndrome. All the above were the thoughts, recollections and reflections which flashed before me as I waited for Trish to tell me about the crisis. I moved to respond to her comments – the ones about my having a problem.

'Let's go back in your room,' I said. We did. 'Now why don't you tell me why I've got a problem? Obviously it's a problem you feel you can't solve, so it's my job to help and I'd like to,' I lied. I have this technique of making superficially appropriate noises whilst embedding my remarks in an ironic framework. Well, that's how I see it. Trish just gave me a funny look. 'You've taken me by surprise,' I said. 'This placement was one I just was not worried about. The school is rock solid. Committed Head and deputy both on board. Sharon is, by any standards, a cracking student and you could scour the region before you found a better mentor than Meg.'

'Not Meg,' said Trish.

I was confused; so much so that I thought for a minute that she'd said nutmeg. Nutmeg is well understood as a spice, but for a bizarre moment I thought she was referring to what I understand is a professional's trick in soccer. It involves, I believe, sticking the ball through a player's legs and running around him. The technical details are unimportant. What matters is that having it done to one is regarded as a minor (at least) humiliation which can lead to a breakdown of relationships between players of opposite teams. I couldn't think what the mentoring equivalent was but there seemed to be plenty of examples. Certainly it seemed that what Trish had just done to me was a particularly good example. However, I'd got it completely wrong about what I'd heard. What Trish had said was, 'Not Meg.'

'Meg went down with a bug just after you'd been talking to Derek Wilson at that meeting. We had to find another mentor.'

Two thoughts sprang immediately into my head, 'Does this mean Sharon's been stuck with a duff mentor?' and 'Why wasn't I told?'

'Why wasn't I told?' I asked and I might have added, 'particularly since I'm the person responsible not only for mentor preparation and training but also the person responsible for negotiating the placements and mentor allocations,' but I didn't. Having let my thoughts run free only moments before complaining about Trish being a 'dumper' I had the uneasy feeling that events had made a monkey of me. I had the strange feeling that she was actually going to say, 'I sorted it all out.'

'I sorted it all out,' said Trish.

I thought to myself that no doubt she had had the assistance of Derek Wilson who I suspected had begun to fancy himself as a DIY teacher trainer. He had shown a passing interest in SCITT at one time.

'Well, Derek Wilson and I sorted it out. We found her another mentor.'

Somehow, I would have expected her to be a little smug about this. But she wasn't; indeed she seemed a little uneasy about the whole thing.

'Who did you get to take her on?' I asked, visions of Tom floating to the front of my mind.

'Mark Bennett,' she said.

Things could be much worse. Mark was the Arts co-ordinator, fairly new to the school and as a result he hadn't actually completed the full diet of mentor preparation and training. He had, however, been a mentor in his previous school, although working to a different scheme with a different university. I remember he'd asked me why we couldn't get our act together with our nextdoor neighbour university. I also remember explaining to him that they had nextdoor neighbours too – apart from us – who themselves had nextdoor neighbours and so on all around the country, each one overlapping with the other – a series of acts to get together. Nonetheless I had found him a personable and likeable young man with an enthusiastic and committed approach to teaching, who could move easily between KS1 and KS2. I knew his wife too. She was one of our mentors. She'd just gone back to teaching, leaving their two young children in the charge of Mum. Mark had told me that he always appreciated having students and found that he learnt from working with them. He had told me that he tried to be very supportive and certainly the evidence pointed that way. I was aware too that he'd been on a course to develop his interpersonal skills, because he intended after a couple of years to apply for a deputy headship. I remember joking with him about it and asking him to exemplify some of the new interpersonal skills he had picked up. He had taken my questionable teasing very seriously and given me the example I'd jokingly asked for.

'I recognise that I need to listen attentively to people if I'm to explore their concerns. I need to make adequate and meaningful eye contact with people.' I'd asked him if it worked and he'd nodded vigorously.

'It works for me,' he said. 'It's given me much more confidence in my relationships with people, at what's been a difficult time in my own life.'

I'd made a mental note that Mark was someone I reckoned I liked who was making all the right noises and I thought no more about his final remark. I smiled brightly at Trish.

'That sounds an excellent choice. He's on the course – the Monday night mentor course – and he's also done the in-service module on interpersonal skills. In fact we were talking about things only a few weeks ago. He's trying hard to develop his interpersonal skills. Taking over from Meg should give him a good opportunity to practise those newly developed interpersonal skills on Sharon.'

Trish looked at me, hard.

'Precisely,' she said, and looked me in the eye.

I began dimly to see what might be coming.

She continued.

'That's when all the trouble started . . . Mark and Sharon really did gel as mentor and mentee. Team teaching, that's what got them interested in devising a way of teaching Shakespeare to Year 2 children. Planning together, sharing an enthusiasm for English Literature, going on the LEA workshop together. Things were really happening in that classroom! Sharon launched a literacy initiative aimed at getting her Year 2 children to develop their independent writing. It went like a bomb. She invented a fictional character who wrote to the children, a huge gerbil called Gertrude, who visited the classroom every night and left notes for the children. The working out of the project in practice was very onerous, but Mark was so supportive that he helped her do these notes every night. Sharon and Mark got on so well! Mark suggested that Gertrude should develop a spelling problem which the children would help her correct – fantastic ideas were coming out of there. Then Sharon suggested that Gertrude had a problem with her digraphs. It was exciting! Year 2 kids could use and understand these grammatical terms, besides which they know loads about gerbils now. Meanwhile, Sharon's file was a dream. Her contextual analysis was so good, that when I showed it to Derek he thought it could be a good basis for the school development plan.'

I shuddered. I could see how the staff would enjoy being set an example by a raw student. Was there no limit to this man's talent for recycling?

Trish pressed on.

'Mark had started to keep his own file, with plans, his own contextual analysis, key features and reflections. He commented regularly in her file. Unfortunately, after a highly intellectual beginning I began to notice some gushy, highly uncritical comments . . . and to cut a long story short, what with notes from hamsters, the Shakespeare project, Sharon's file, Mark's file and more and more discussions, later and later into the evening, suddenly, it was an Apollo 13 syndrome: "Houston, we have a problem!"'

I looked at her hard. Impressed as I was by the model of dedicated mentoring she had outlined, I could see that the storm clouds were gathering. Possibly the storm was raging already.

'Spell it out for me,' I demanded. 'Smoke? Fire? Who knows what? Who's doing what?'

'More smoke than fire,' said Trish, 'working well into the evening – together – preparing and talking, vibrations of intimacy, repairing to the local Pizza Hut for coffee, innocent handholding. These are the public sightings. As to knowledge and action, basically Derek has talked to Mark. Mark recognises that he is playing with fire, and may well get his fingers burnt, but it appears he is not a happy man. He and Sue, his wife, have two small children and he has a wounded ego. He reckons he's been playing second fiddle to them for two or three years. He thinks he for his part has been building a career and could have done with more support. Now Sue has gone back to teaching and her mother who's looking after the toddlers seems to be in the house more and more. Sue comes back tired and then follow a few hours of family chaos. Mark has begun to find his own extended school day mentoring Sharon a recurring oasis of peace and tranquillity: interesting career-enhancing work with someone to whom he can talk about the job, and who thinks he's wonderfully supportive, helpful and focused on her and her needs. He's heard what Derek has said. He doesn't like it, but he can see what's at stake.'

'And?'

'Meg came back yesterday. At first Mark assumed that he'd see the mentor's job out for the rest of the placement – two weeks and a day – but now after talking to Derek, he's reluctantly accepted that Meg should take over. For public consumption she's finishing what she started and in any case, technically, she's the approved, i.e. qualified, mentor. But he's not happy.'

'Well, tough,' I said. When Trish had been talking I'd recalled Mark's casual – or so I had thought – comment to me weeks ago, about a difficult time in his life. Obviously problems at home had been building up, but even recognising as I did the circumstances which had caused the problem, and although cherishing a soft spot for love's young dream, and being, as I believed, worldly wise and tolerant, I was not happy either. Oddly enough, it was not Mark's two small children and overworked wife holding down two jobs that I was bothered about. It was our student, Sharon. He'd really messed her up. I recognised the position I was taking and I spelt it out to Trish.

'It's Sharon I'm bothered about,' I confessed. 'She's so good, she was doing so well and now she's plunged into turmoil. It's funny isn't it? We tell the schools that the interests of the children come first. It's even written into the Partnership Agreement – "Clause 3.2.1 – the welfare of pupils in schools will override all other considerations" – I helped frame it myself. Well, there are no children in that school involved here directly, but the way I look at it is this: the students we have are *our* pupils. We are responsible for them. We must look out for their welfare. Quite apart from all the talking which has to be done, as far as the placement is concerned, the sooner Meg takes over the better.'

Trish was looking at me with some embarrassment. 'It's a little more complicated than that.'

'How complicated?' I said, feeling irritation mounting, although I was far from clear as to precisely what it was I was irritated about or with whom I was irritated.

Trish dropped her bombshell. 'Derek thinks we should pull Sharon out of the school.'

'What did you say to that?' I asked, but suspecting what was coming and staring at the D branded on her forehead. D for Dumper.

'I said I'd come and talk it over with you. I'm afraid I might have hinted that I agreed with him. I hadn't seen it from the angle you've just taken.'

'Sharon . . . ', I said, slowly and calmly – as I believed – but emphasising each word in what was probably my best patronising manner, 'Sharon is *our* student. We have to consider *her* welfare. She is on a placement. The school agreed to take her. The school agreed to mentor her. Admittedly Meg's illness was unpredictable. Admittedly a good solution, or what appeared as a good solution, was found. Now it's all gone pear-shaped. Sharon is an extremely talented, able young woman, lively, bubbly, personable, yes attractive too, but she is also very immature about personal relationships and she is very naive. She seems to have fallen for some doe-eyed predatory wimp, if you can have such a thing, who is offloading all his domestic and personal career problems on to her. It's pathetic; he's pathetic.' All my previous kind thoughts about Mark had vanished in a puff of smoke, with or without fire. 'Now you're suggesting that she leaves school with her tail between her legs. Does she want to leave?'

'No, to be fair,' said Trish, 'but I haven't actually talked to her about it all very much. I didn't want to say the wrong thing. I was sure that you'd be talking to her.'

By now I was beady eyed and I bored into her with those beady eyes as she shuffled uncomfortably. I knew what lay ahead: hours of anguished discussion, with Sharon, with Derek and with Meg. For the latter two I'd have to go to the school. Sharon, I could talk to that same evening. She was due back for a meeting and I would separate her from the rest and we'd talk it through. It might yet have an upside. This was her first real setback; it might well be her first real emotional trauma too. I knew I had to put the pieces together again and she might emerge stronger for it. I was sure I could mend her. The qualities she had, did not, in my view, derive from superficial talents. Sharon was strong inside and out; it would be a mess, but we'd sort it out. As to Derek, I could, I believed, handle Derek. He wouldn't want a 'failure', for that is how Sharon's departure would seem, and I'd make sure it did seem like that. Moreover, he knew the score. He would agree with me that Mark was in the wrong. Sharon was no smouldering seductress who had set her cap at him. In any case, I knew he liked and admired Sharon's work. He'd had good feedback from staff and parents, so just so long as there wasn't any serious parent 'aggro' in all this, then all would be well. I wondered who exactly had seen them at the Pizza Hut, and that wondering gave me a small *frisson*, but I gathered that so far this was no *cause célèbre*. Shame about Mark! I'd felt he was better than that and I did feel sorry for him underneath my crossness. However, I had a plan. Meg worked with Relate. She would sort it out. She was perfectly placed to get Mark and his wife back on track. The next day when I put this to her, her reaction left me in no doubt that I should stick to school liaison, placements, working with mentors, homespun philosophy and firefighting.

'You're off your head,' she said. 'I'll work with Sharon, as a mentor, and if she wants to talk to me about her personal problems, I'll try to separate those out, but I'm not promising. What counts for me is how she works with my children in my classroom.'

I thought back to my attitude the previous day when I had been so protective of Sharon.

Meg continued, 'That's what comes first for me. But don't worry, I'll look after Sharon and I'll do everything I can, but I am not, absolutely not, embarking on marriage guidance counselling with a colleague. It would be totally inappropriate. I just don't do that,' she said. Then she paused, and smiled, 'but I know a man who does! I'll put Mark in touch with someone from Relate.'

I was content with that, but was left licking my mental wounds at being exposed as a meddling, albeit well-meaning, amateur. All I wanted was for all of them to live happily ever after. But that conversation with Meg lay in the future. There I was back with Trish contemplating the work I knew I had to do now that the perfect placement had gone wrong. Trish looked relieved when I explained what I was proposing. I'd sort it out; that was what I was proposing. Trish liked that idea. She changed tack.

'When I was looking for you before and we bumped into each other in the corridor, you were about to say something weren't you?' Trish asked, 'What was it?'

'Just routine,' I said, 'I was going to tell you about this session's inspection'.

'Not again!' said Trish. 'They're never out of the place. What is it this time?'

I gave her a Paddington Bear-style hard stare. 'They're looking at mentor preparation and training,' I said, 'and they will be concentrating on personal, social and moral education. They particularly want to know how we help mentors support students in what is, and I quote, "a difficult and challenging" area.'

'Will you be organising a meeting about it?' asked Trish.

'I expect so.' I sighed. 'When I've got time'.

COMMENTARY AND MATTERS FOR DISCUSSION

Gender

The complication in this tale is the attraction between Mark and Sharon. That gender is a factor affecting the mentoring process is acknowledged by Reich (1995) in a study in a business context. He found that women benefit from informal mentoring relationships and that on the whole women benefit from more intangible support as well as concrete aid. Reich also found that men's and women's approaches to mentoring differed and that for women the affective, or emotional, quality was more important. In tune with this research, the Manchester project identified as important the closeness of the mentor–mentee relationship, a factor commented on by same-gender pairs and mixed-gender pairs. Problem areas included the difficulties of being 'objective', of giving constructive feedback which might contain negative comments, of making the mentees aware that their performance was not good enough. It would appear that in mixed-gender pairs, gender awareness and early discussion of equal opportunity issues, such as those related to stereotypical views of female teachers, are a prerequisite for all mentors. In 'Mentors' stories' (see Chapter 7) Tom returns to this issue directly and the Mark/Sharon case study is further explored. A discussion about, and an agreed definition of, professional behaviour would also help to highlight problematical areas. The issue of gender in mentoring might be thought to be similar to one related to co-educational or single-sex schooling. Who benefits most? It would appear from both Reich's (1995) and Campbell and Kane's (1996b) research that men can reasonably justify learning more from being mentored by a woman, because women are better 'equipped' for sharing and talking about their experiences. Many justifications for co-educational schools fall into the same category: for example, that girls make the school atmosphere more pleasant and keep the boys' behaviour in check. It would be useful to hear more arguments about the benefits of mixed-gender mentoring and to explore what the experience has to offer to teachers' professional development.

In the Mentoring in Schools project there can be little doubt that the school in which these problems were raised experienced a sharp focus on issues related to gender, which hopefully informed both thinking and practice in mentoring. Issues related to managing staff relationships, developing a code of behaviour and managing delicate situations would clearly feature as areas for exploration in the future, as might discussion about stereotyping of male and female behaviour. The particular gender composition of the normal primary school – mostly staffed by female teachers – surprisingly does not seem to counter the development of stereotypical views about teachers' and student teachers' behaviour. Is sexism so ingrained in society that even those disadvantaged by it perpetuate the discriminatory behaviour? Mixed-gender mentoring may serve to highlight these issues and bring them into the arena for debate.

Challenge and support

Sharon liked to be challenged and needed to be challenged. Meg revealed great strength as a mentor who was prepared to challenge. Although there were contextual complications, it would appear that Mark, too, had the capacity to move students on to the next level. It is not always so.

There is evidence to suggest that mentors often fail to challenge student teachers in their discussions about teaching. Daloz (1986) refers to the characteristics of support and challenge and discusses how support can be seen as an affirming activity and as evidence of care which a teacher might feel towards a student. Challenge on the other hand is often perceived as a negative activity which 'peels boundaries apart' instead of bringing them together. Cameron-Jones and O'Hara (1997) in their study of teachers mentoring students found that even when teachers felt they were emphasising challenge with their students, so low was the level of challenge that the students were unaware of being challenged. This study also asserts that there is little evidence to be found of the crucial combination of support and challenge in school-based teacher education. This assertion is countered by Dunne and Bennett (1997). Their findings, in a study of mentoring processes in pre-service training, were arrived at through analyses of the perspectives of, and the dialogues between, student teachers and all those involved in their mentoring institution and its partner schools. They found little support for previous empirical claims that dialogues between students and mentors are characterised by a lack of challenge and reflection. They believe that mentors are capable of challenge but that the process of challenge should be facilitated in structural ways. Whether immersion in the school context provides the best learning experience, and what models of mentoring promote the best quality learning for pre-service teachers, are questions they highlighted.

The model of mentoring which lies beneath Sharon's tale began with that of a class teacher who is supporting the student, as the official mentor. In this tale, as suggested above, the person has much to offer. That model is certainly not the only model available. Its weakness is the unlikelihood of finding sufficient class teachers able and willing to go beyond the 'support' role and into 'challenge' territory; in which case, how can 'challenge' be built into mentoring?

A variant could include having in the school one person designated as 'lead' mentor, moderating, standardising, and generally facilitating the evolution of school-based training in that school. Arguably, therefore, that semi-external person could be the key mentor on whom the university bestowed formally the additional role to challenge or extend or at least raise developmental issues by intervening in a structured way in the direct relationship between class teacher mentor and student. Such a person would progressively gain more and more experience on a longitudinal basis, i.e. term-on-term, year-on-year, and could be consciously 'developed' by the university. However, this superficially attractive solution causes other problems to arise. The essential mentor relationship is likely to remain between the student and class teacher. Since time for mentor development, which also has a financial cost, is a scarce resource, it is arguable that such time as any university has for development work might more appropriately be targeted upon working up the strengths of class teacher mentors rather than in developing a 'super-mentor'. Moreover, it is questionable how much time the 'super-mentor' might have available. It is conceivable that the number of visits, follow-up discussions and de-briefings which could be carried out might actually be little more than was the case under old-fashioned arrangements when university tutors did that job. Almost certainly, the issue has become academic, now that more and more primary school deputy heads – the obvious candidates for 'super-mentorship' – have returned to substantial class-based duties as budget shares shrink and deficits rise. Finally a question has to be asked about what happens as mentors move on. This issue of mentor turnover is discussed further in later tales. The issue of support and challenge is also raised in the commentary section in Paula's story.

Furlong and Maynard (1993) warn of the dangers of students 'hitting the plateau' and not being challenged by mentors to develop further, resulting in a complacency about teaching and a lack of rigour in supervision.

The dialogue between teacher mentors and their mentees is obviously of crucial importance in the process of mentoring. Edwards and Collison (1996), in their study of conversations before and after student teaching, would suggest the cruciality of higher-education-led seminar sessions which allow for wider ranging, more general conversations which are not 'limited by the fact that they are so often tightly connected to the implementation of classroom tasks for pupils'. This is a powerful argument for structuring courses in such a way that there is good opportunity for students to 'leave the battlefield', draw breath and think through their experiences. Edwards and Collison found little evidence of mentors encouraging students to think critically. This is not necessarily at odds with Dunne and Bennett (1997), who believe that such challenge can be found in mentoring and can be done by mentors but must be built into the model.

Edwards and Collison identified a reduction in risk-taking, with students and teachers engaging in 'bidding down' classroom tasks undertaken by students sometimes as a strategy to avoid failure. There is a great deal of pressure to engineer unproblematic situations and to have students 'fit in' with the host teacher's practice. Yet working with able students requires teachers to be prepared to take risks and to extend their mentoring skills. McIntyre and Hagger (1993) discuss levels of mentoring and stress the need for 'developed mentoring' where collaborative teaching is a major focus and for 'extended mentoring' where there is a transition to a new kind of relationship. This is not always easy. Whole-school mentoring approaches and issues which draw on sources of knowledge outside the school to provide learning are features of this 'extended mentoring' phase which can challenge and stimulate both teachers and students.

What makes a good mentor? Towards an answer

Meg, it was claimed by the narrator, was a fine mentor. Questionable behaviour apart, Mark was represented in the tale as a good mentor.

What is a good mentor? In Chapter 6, 'Triumph and disaster' students' views are examined. There are views too in the literature. Much investigation of the role of mentor, e.g. Devlin (1995), Fish (1995a), Turner (1995), Tomlinson (1995), stresses the importance of interpersonal skills. 'Getting on' with one's mentor is at the foremost of most student teachers' minds as they embark upon a block placement, and failure to do so can seriously affect progress in teaching (see the commentary on mentors' stories in Chapter 7 for yet another perspective on mentors' roles and responsibilities.) Bonding between mentor and student is a delicate affair, requiring the making of a relationship which on a daily basis spans both the professional and personal aspects of life, and one which mentors find challenging and at times frustrating. Teachers' attitudes to the 'ownership' of classrooms, pupils and student teachers, raise issues of influence and control. Teachers often feel a sense of loss with regard to their pupils when students take their class and often resist any activities which take them away from their classes for more than half a day. This is revealed as an issue in Chapter 6, 'Triumph and disaster'.

Mentoring is different from teaching but it is not the same as counselling. It demands an impressive command of a wide range of skills covering good communication, time management, open-mindedness, and an ability to model. Edwards and Collison (1996) remind us that 'active mentoring' is not simply a question of transferring skills used with children and applying them to students. Furlong and Maynard (1995), in their concluding remarks at the end of their account of a research project, stress the key issues regarding the mentor's role, 'Mentoring strategies must be built upon an informed understanding of how students learn and on a clear vision of the forms of professionalism they are trying to engender.'

'Getting too close to your mentee' has been identified as problematic, Campbell and Kane (1996a), and many mentors feel that it is useful to keep some distance between themselves and the student. One Project mentor had definite views: 'I've always maintained that a good mentor needs to be slightly detached. There are certain aspects, if you get too close, that are difficult to tackle.' Another mentor found that the role of being a friendly supporter who also gave challenges, and who was more objective because of the distance, resulted in considerable benefits in the mentoring of students. However, it is the role of assessor which seems to generate tension. This has been explored fully in Mike's tale and in the subsequent commentary, but it is interesting to raise the question of what would have happened if Mark had been in the situation of having to assess Sharon, with perhaps her degree classification resting on that assessment.

Priorities

'It's Sharon I'm bothered about,' I confessed. 'She's so good. She was doing so well and now she's plunged into turmoil! It's funny isn't it? We tell the schools that the interests of the children come first. It's even written into the Partnership Agreement – "Clause 3.2.1 – the welfare of the pupils in schools will override all other considerations" – I helped frame it myself. Well, there are no children in that school involved here directly, but the way I look at it is this: the students we have are our *pupils*. We are responsible for them.'

The conflict of interests of university tutors, such as the narrator who is also the placement tutor, and school mentors is neatly summarised in the above quotation – a real dilemma of partnership schemes. It is doubtful whether the narrator's analogy is strictly accurate. Certainly there is a sense in which university tutors must look to the welfare of their students in the same way that class teachers, mentors, head teachers, and others in the school must look to the welfare of the children at all times. There should always be someone who 'stands for' the student – they are not always in the wrong! However, the student is not a student in the abstract. He or she is a student of something, in this case of education and teaching, while preparing to become a teacher. It is a non-negotiable part of the teacher's role to exercise 'due care' and 'due diligence'. What complicates the issues in this little tale, however, is uncertainty about whether the children were being put at risk. It would appear that they were getting a very good deal. Two teachers were working excessive overtime to their pupils' certain benefit. The fact that their energies were being fuelled by something additional to professional commitment was a problem for the school and its staff. A problem also for other 'stakeholders' was whether they should have become aware of it. Whatever harm was being done was not demonstrably being done to the children. Damage was arising largely at the personal level with the meeting point the area of interpersonal relationships within the school. Thus, showing the red card to Sharon, which could have been professionally, and maybe personally destructive for her, was not the easy solution it appeared. Should Trish have known this? Arguably, yes, but certainly there was a case for having someone protect Sharon's interest – as opposed to 'the school's'. The concept of 'the school's interest' is not necessarily the same as 'the children's interest.' In that sense the narrator's point is well made. The 'realpolitik' of partnership is, however, such that it would take a strong-minded tutor *and* a school with a well-developed sense of the concept of partnership to solve or resolve the issue in a way which left all the pieces on the board.

FURTHER READING

Issues of challenge and support are discussed more fully in the following:

Daloz, L. (1986) *Effective Teaching and Mentoring*. San Francisco: Jossey Bass.
Cameron-Jones, M. and O'Hara, P. (1997) 'Support and challenge in teacher education', *British Educational Research Journal* **23**(1), 15–26.

For a detailed examination of mentoring conversations and of mentoring in action, Chapters 3 and 4 of Edwards, A. and Collison, J. (1996) *Mentoring and Developing Practice in Primary Schools*, Milton Keynes: Open University Press, is entirely useful and thought-provoking.

'Getting too close' and 'Keeping your distance' are discussed more fully in Campbell, A. and Kane, I. (1996a) 'Mentoring and primary school culture', in McIntyre, D. and Hagger, H. (eds) *Mentors in Schools: Developing the Profession of Teaching*, London: David Fulton Publishers.

Reich, M. (1995) 'The mentor connection' in Kerry, T. and Shelton Mayes, A. (eds) *Issues in Mentoring*, London: Routledge, raises the issue of gender and its relationship to mentoring, albeit in a business context, but there are common issues with mentoring in an education context.

A good discussion of issues concerning the identification of good teaching is contained within Chapter 2 of Brown, S. and McIntyre, D. (1993) *Making Sense of Teaching*, Milton Keynes: Open University Press. Chapter 3 discusses how teachers talk about their good teaching and goes some way to exploring how to gain access to teachers' 'tacit professional knowledge'.

CHAPTER 5

Out of the mouths: child's eye views

Wilma arrived for her MEd tutorial with a wicked gleam in her eye.

'I've finished them,' she said. 'Have *I* got news for you!'

I was momentarily nonplussed, but then I quickly remembered what it was we were going to talk about. I have explained before that Wilma's 'practitioner enquiry' was about mentoring and she had been developing a number of intriguing lines of investigation. At the last tutorial she had said something odd.

'Mentoring is all about the grown-ups isn't it? How to do it; who to do it to; who does it; what does x think? Teachers, tutors, students, head teachers, parents, governors – they all get their say, and throughout it all we all say that the children must come first. But, in fact, we never actually ask the children do we? We never get their slant on what's happening with all the students coming in and out. And what is happening? Is it one long round of teachers and teaching with the names and faces changed? Do they like all this fuss? Normally, I reckon kids like visitors, and like new faces, but the other week, I'd gone in to watch David. As it happened Damien, the class teacher, was in the stockroom popping in and out, then in walked your Trish. Derek was with her. He never leaves her alone. He's terrified about OFSTED and assessment, recording and reporting and now he's found out that she's a super expert he thinks he's won the lottery. Anyway, in they came – five adults: me, David, Damien, Derek, Trish. I thought at the time that we only needed one of your teacher-training inspectors plus an external examiner and we'd got the Magnificent Seven. Then, blow me, there's a dull thud and there's the window cleaner polishing away. Super Eight. All this bunch crowding out the classroom – except the window cleaner of course who was the only one the kids were paying attention to – and all because of mentoring. My conclusion was that if *I* were a kid, I'd be shouting out "invasion of privacy". I'd down tools and bunk off. Well, of course, that's all a bit of an exaggeration, but it got me thinking about what it might all seem like to the children.'

'Why don't you find out?' I'd suggested. 'Ask them. It's pretty much unexplored territory.'

So she'd done just that and that night she was going to tell me about it. We'd worked out a framework. The children in Years 5 and 6 were to be asked to comment about the benefits and disadvantages of having student teachers working in their classrooms, about the length of time they spent with the particular class and about the activities and teaching they provided. We'd come up with a few broad headings which Wilma was going to try to group comments under. Wilma's list was:

- student behaviour and characteristics,
- perceptions of higher education tutors, and mentors,
- managing and organising students,
- teachers and students: what's the difference?

'There's some rum stuff in this,' said Wilma. 'Bits of it have just left me gob-smacked. You can see how easily I drop into kid-talk.'

'Good news or bad?' I enquired.

'Bit of both really. Mixed. I laughed more than you will.'

She'd concentrated mainly on Year 6 and on one student: the one whose class had been invaded, David Brown. She was David's mentor and the class teacher he was attached to was Damien. I can't remember Damien's surname mainly because it is of Polish origin and I have the standard British citizen's facility with languages and keep making a fool of myself. The children used to get their tongues round it, but David Brown was certainly a lot easier for me. Wilma was actually teaching the parallel Year 6 class. David was a freshly minted postgraduate for whom the phrase 'bright-eyed and bushy-tailed' might have been personally invented. Mainly he veered between enthusiastic and excitable but occasionally he would have a go at being cool and laid back. I'd seen him teach once on one of my 'pastoral visits', but his supervising tutor was Trish. She quite rated him and she actually gushed about the class.

'They're lovely,' she said once. 'I love going in and now and again working with a group. David seems to welcome that too. It shares the load and makes him feel like a co-professional. He enjoys it.'

'I'm sure he does,' I'd said.

David's degree was in Geography, but he hadn't been anywhere much, apart from field trips to Whitby. He'd gone straight to university from school and straight on to a PGCE course from his degree. All his part-time jobs had been pubs or parks and gardens. He had quite a lot of knowledge, but not a lot of experience. Still, there didn't appear to have been much wrong with the practice. I could sense Wilma was bursting to tell me what she'd found.

She interrupted my reverie. 'Let's start with student behaviour and characteristics.'

'Let's do that,' I smiled.

'I reckon,' said Wilma 'that the thing students have got going for them is youth.'

I winced.

'Students also seem to have some sort of special entertainment value and a sense of humour is essential. I've decided you should put that in your admissions policy. Judging mainly by David, although the same sort of comments came out of the other classes which have had students recently, they're also seen to be more approachable and friendly. There seems to be a fair chance that if they overdo that bit, then it isn't appreciated. The kids see it for what it is and it can backfire. I suppose I'm talking generally here, but I can see big hints of it in the comments I've got. Basically, though, students have a novelty value which works best to their advantage when they bring new ideas into the classroom. I suppose that's where you tutors come in. I've got loads of quotes and masses of stuff on the tapes, but let me read you just a few.'

She did:

- 'Students should be fun, understanding and they should like children. I'd prefer them to be young, so they've still got some fun left in them, and when they still make an effort to understand us and still like children.'
- 'They should be strict but with a good sense of humour. I think students are much more fun than ordinary teachers.'
- 'Students act differently when their tutor is around. They laugh and talk more when the tutor is not around.'
- 'Students always have good ideas.'
- 'They are softer on pupils.'
- 'They tend to be more creative and more fun.'

'Did you spot the schizophrenia?' she concluded. 'They transmogrify when you lot come in. I'll have more to say about that later.' The last sentence was in her best pseudo-lecturer tone. I was beginning to get a hint of what was coming later.

'So,' I said, 'you're beginning to conclude that there are key differences in the perceptions children have as between student teachers and "real" teachers?'

'I don't think I'd put it quite so pretentiously – sorry, clinically – as that, but yes. Listen to these comments:

"To be a good teacher you need a good mix of everything, not just being completely strict."

"It's better than I thought, having a student, because it's not like having a proper teacher, because proper teachers stay with you for a whole year, and if you don't like the teacher then it's just tough luck, but if you don't like the student, well OK."

"I think students are more like friends than real teachers."

"I don't think students have as much respect and sometimes children don't treat them like teachers."

"The students don't have as much control over the class as teachers do and they lose their temper much quicker."

"They're not like ordinary teachers, like Mr Karcewski, he's always tired and strict and bad tempered. Students are more like friends than real teachers, though sometimes they try to be like those teachers you see on TV – like telling somebody off all the time."

"I think students always have good ideas and are more creative than our teachers. I really liked it when we were allowed to bring in all our CDs and tapes to do a project on the media, but Mr Karcewski went and spoilt it all by saying Oasis weren't in the National Curriculum, so we had to change to Mozart or something. How boring! Nobody's heard of them."'

Wilma now lapsed into pseudo-lecturer mode again.

'It would appear,' she said, 'that pupils perceive students as different from teachers, sometimes implying less value with regard to learning and more value with regard to fun. This provides an interesting insight into how children separate enjoyment and learning in their experience of school. Perhaps one of the challenges for school-based teacher education is to link the experience of learning with that of enjoyment in more pupils' minds.'

And she called *me* pretentious! But I could see what she was getting at. Quite apart from other considerations, students need to develop their image as teachers. 'Is this because they are called students,' I wondered or were there very different reasons, such as children's ability to pressure students, and often new teachers, to establish the limits in classrooms. Either way, I couldn't see that, for example, calling them trainees rather than students would help. I've never subscribed to any nominalist fallacy but even setting that aside, for me 'student' still has connotations of higher education, to which I really believe the profession of teaching should be linked. 'Trainees' was something else again.

'Are you still listening?' asked Wilma. 'Shall I go on? I thought you might like to hear how Years 5 and 6 think you should be organising school-based training and what they think some of the issues are.'

'By all means,' I waved my hand in a gesture of assent. I was beginning to enjoy Wilma's presentation. It made a change from aspirant post-modernism or 'What I did last Tuesday with Year 4 and why I think it didn't work out.'

'It would appear, you will be glad to know, that most of the children approve of and accept having students in school. They seem to appreciate the 'extra pair of hands' and acknowledge the extra attention they can get. They quite like that scheme where groups of students come into the same class. Some think it's better than having one teacher in a class because they get to talk about things a lot more. There is, however, a Big Issue for some and I think militant, hooligan behaviour could be on the cards. Let me play you this.'

She fished out the portable recorder. This was clearly something I needed to hear live. A child's voice spoke out clearly.

'Do you know something else? My cousin's a student teacher and she says that students don't get paid for teaching us! It's a scandal. They're probably all starving, with no money. I think we should do something about that. How about we have a campaign or a petition in school and maybe we can talk to the TV news or write to the newspapers. Mr Brown would like that – it would fit in with our project on the media. Mr Brown did say we should fight back about things we feel strongly about.'

'I'll kill him,' I said calmly.

'Fortunately,' Wilma consoled me, 'there are milder more rational voices, concerned with day-to-day practicalities.'

'Such wisdom,' I murmured.

'Here we are,' said Wilma and read from her notes:

- '"I think we should maybe have one student per year. It is fair that they don't get paid – because they are training."
- "I think five weeks is too long to have a student – one week is about enough."
- "We should have students once a year."
- "I think it's a good idea to have lots of students to help out."
- "They should do more lessons and give the teacher a rest."
- "I would rather have groups of students than just one – you get more attention."
- "I think there should be more student teachers and they should not be paid. The money should go to real teachers."'

'And their tutors,' I added. 'Oh wise and learned kid.'

'I've got some stuff about tutors. I've been saving it,' Wilma smiled. 'You can work it in to your evaluation. It's all good illuminative stuff. That's what you call it isn't it, when you make it up as you go along?'

'Something like that.' I spoke through clenched teeth and displayed a wan, forced smile.

Wilma cleared her throat, 'The following observations were made about the higher education tutors and their visits which, of course, we in schools all welcome.

- "I don't think tutors should come in to school. It puts off students and children. It also makes the student act differently, to try to impress their tutors, perhaps."
- "When he was on his own in class he wasn't making much effort but when his tutor was in he made a really big effort and tried to do everything right."
- "When the tutor comes in to check on the student teacher, they most of the time act differently. They don't tell jokes and aren't as much fun."
- "I find it difficult to concentrate on my work when the tutor is in, because I feel she is watching me."

- "I don't like tutors, they make you feel as if you're in an exam."
- "Mr Brown was different when the lady tutor was in, you know the one I mean, always asking us what we were doing and if we understood it. Why can't she keep out of it and mind her own business? Yuk, she had too much perfume on, I nearly threw up. Mr Brown didn't act like he did when he was on his own. He didn't tell any jokes and she wasn't much fun."
- "My student was really lazy except when the tutor was coming – we had a man tutor and all he did was sit in the corner and stare at us all, and read the student's file. I had a look at the file once, and the tutor had written all over it in red pen. I don't think our student was doing very well. She wasn't much good at teaching science – couldn't keep us in order – she was too soft; she needs to get a bit tougher with us."
- "I think it might be better if we could write a report on students and then the tutor wouldn't need to come into the classroom. It might be best if the tutor actually watched the student from outside the classroom."
- "I don't rate our student anyway. Not in Year 6. I reckon he should go down to Year 3. Then that woman tutor can go and smarm around the little kids."'

'It's not easy,' I said, 'coming into a strange situation and trying to be unobtrusive.'

'It's not,' agreed Wilma. 'How's this for unobtrusive? I've saved it till the end.

- "One day a complete stranger came in and sat at the back of Mr Brown's room. Mr Brown said this was a Very Important Person and we were all to be very well-behaved. If we were we could have quizzes all afternoon. If we weren't he'd kill us. All because of this Person. All the Person did was sit at the back, write in a big black notebook and glare at us. I wouldn't like to be in that Person's class – seemed really, really horrible. We all cheered when the door closed. Mr Brown cheered as well."'

'And this was when?' I asked gently.

'Last week.'

'And this "Person" was?'

'Well, it was you, wasn't it?'

I decided to reserve my defence. I did not share the image the children had of me. They had got it wrong.

'What do you make of all that then?' I asked, distancing myself from the action.

'Well,' said Wilma, 'I think kids these days are SATs-hardened and they're well used to a variety of teacher assessment procedures. As a result they're very quick to spot an assessment situation. Thus they easily discern when student behaviour becomes markedly different in the presence of the tutor. In fact, it's clear that several of the children felt under examination themselves and found it difficult to concentrate. Somehow, I think that if you lot are going to keep coming in, we're going to have to find a way to negotiate a role within the classroom and some means by which the children can relate to the tutor, otherwise that Person is just going to be seen as supervisory, inspectorial and judgemental.'

I bridled. 'What about mentors? Aren't they judgemental, as well as supervisory?'

Wilma wrinkled her brow. 'I'm not sure,' she said. 'If I'm to be involved more and more in the assessment, how does that affect my capacity to point out weaknesses and help the students improve? There's a dual role – a clash.'

'Same problem we've had for years,' I said sympathetically. 'It's a line you have to learn to draw.' I was dipping in to my collection of useful clichés. 'There *is* a tension. You do what you can to help but then, in the end, if the student's no good, he or she fails. It's like your MEd thesis,' I said, mischievously. 'I'll do everything I can to help you make it a masterpiece but in the end, if it's full of libellous material about me, it'll fail.'

'Fair enough,' said Wilma. 'I can now see that the task of the tyro mentor is through experience and scholarship to mature into the role of wise counsellor and objective assessor.'

'Precisely. Do you have more pearls of wisdom?'

'Just a few – hard to classify – a mixture of helpful hints, educational philosophy, and the application of assessment criteria against the competences set out in Circular 14/93.'

'Forget them,' I said, 'there's a new lot coming out, called Standards.'

'What's the difference?'

'Not sure, but there's more of them and they're going to transform teacher education and training.'

'Do the children need to know?'

'Do they know about Circular 14/93?'

'No.'

'Well then.'

'What about the career entry profiles?'

'They'll change too. You'll have to come to terms with a new set of jargon.'

'I can hardly wait,' sighed Wilma, 'but meantime you might like to add the following to whatever they should be added to.' She read out:

- '"I like the way Mr Brown works but it could be improved by marking our work in the proper way with a red pen rather than writing nice comments that don't say what's wrong with the work."
- "To be a good teacher they need to have a mix of everything, not just be strict

or be completely soft and not let some of the kids get away with talking all the time."

- "Mr Brown had his pets which I didn't think was fair, and sometimes he used bad language, like we do in the playground, sort of slang. Teachers should not use slang, or bad language. People who train them should have taught them that."
- "He needs to improve his science teaching. We didn't learn anything new, all we did was copied from the board – I don't think he knew as much as Mr Karcewski about electricity. He looked as though he couldn't fix a plug, and I think he was lucky not to electrocute himself."
- "I liked it when we had easy work, 'cause we got it nearly all right, and then he would read all the answers out slowly so we had time to write them down."'

I responded quickly. 'I've been chewing over some of those comments while we've been talking and thinking about the way everything changes in teacher education fairly regularly. For example, we had one set of criteria in 1984 then it all changed in 1989. In 1992 we began to get into this school-based training, so we got Circular 14/93. Now it's all going to change again in 1997. That's thirteen years and kids who were in Year 6 in 1984 will be 23, 24 now, except they weren't in Year 6 then, they were in Junior 4. So, in my confusion, my conclusion is that what your children have to say has one overriding advantage.'

'What's that?' asked Wilma.

'Eternal wisdom. Come on, let's go to the pub and talk about mentoring.'

COMMENTARY AND MATTERS FOR DISCUSSION

Students and teaching

Little has been written about how primary school children experience partnership ventures in teacher education, or how children feel about having another 'teacher' in the class. This lack of pupil involvement in partnership is acknowledged by Stoll and Fink (1996). They make a case for involving pupils in the improvement process and in partnership ventures, although they identify that many teachers are resistant to any notion of partnership which includes pupils. There have been approaches to investigating pupils' attitudes to schooling. Creative ways of administering 'ethos indicators' to elicit young children's attitudes to school have been developed in Scotland by MacBeath (1994). The way students are introduced to children is subject to variation, some teachers introducing them as students, some as teachers, some as helpers – but what does seem to matter is the status which the teacher and the school gives to students. Temporary staff, including supply teachers, have to work hard to establish themselves and their authority with pupils. Pupils, even very young ones, often see a new face as an opportunity to play up and misbehave. Students have problems in establishing themselves, when they try to emulate teachers' warm and close relationships with pupils, not realising the hard work and tribulations which have gone before, when teachers had to establish their authority.

How much does it matter how the student is introduced to children? In Chapter 6, 'Triumphs and disasters', the status of students as learners is discussed and the point made that the students need to be recognised by the school and the mentor as learners with learners' needs. Regarding them as 'real teachers' does not necessarily assist their learning. But is it helpful if pupils see the student as a learner? Does it affect authority in the classroom? Furlong and Maynard (1995), found that pupils often made students become the sort of teacher they did not want to be, in order to survive. The power of pupil opinion and the manipulation of student teachers is a delicate area, less researched in primary schools, but worthy of further study. The work of Carney and Hagger (1996) and Brown and McIntyre (1993) listed in the further reading section is based on secondary pupils' views of students and teachers, some of which arose from the Oxford Internship Scheme. It is nonetheless illuminating.

The emphasis children put on the youth of students is interesting as pupils often equate youth with fun and enthusiasm. On the whole, children in the Mentoring in Schools Project viewed youthfulness as a positive factor, perhaps indicating that they found it easier to identify with someone closer to their age group. The 'entertainment value' of students should also be noted. The importance of humour in the classroom is generally accepted, but it is also regarded as a risky area for beginning teachers and one which should be approached with caution until the children are better known. Woods and Jeffrey (1996) are concerned that 'the tone of classroom life' should be conducive to children's learning and bemoan the current emphasis upon utilitarianism and 'the close delineation of ends to be achieved, summative assessment with which to measure success, and bureaucratic structures and processes with which to monitor the system'. They worry that 'teaching is in danger of losing its emotional heart'. They advocate the use of humour and metaphor to generate different atmospheres for activities in the classroom. Moyles (1995: 256) also recognises the value of humour in her 'recipe for the perfect teacher' in which she says, 'To my mind, this (recipe) shows just the kind of warmth, humour and beliefs about primary teaching which characterise the new teachers of tomorrow through a balanced and supportive teacher education programme'.

Perhaps the children are identifying a need for those who direct and oversee teacher training, and have national responsibility for it, to revisit the centrality and importance of the affective domain in schools and teaching. It is in danger of being lost. Current initiatives in this area include the US programme, Investing in Excellence (IIE) from the Pacific Institute in Seattle (1997). There are in existence a number of pilot projects looking at how IIE can promote positive self image and self efficacy in teachers.

Children may see students as having 'good ideas for teaching', and rather different approaches to activities than 'real' teachers. They are probably imagining it! By contrast, Furlong and Maynard (1995) discuss 'good ideas for teaching' and assert that teachers are experts in designing these and they use and develop their pedagogical subject knowledge as they go along. They found that students by contrast relied heavily on the 'ready-made' activities they were familiar with from previous experience or from their own schooling.

The children consulted in the project seem to have had experience of fairly enterprising students. Edwards and Knight (1994) write about how teachers and students 'measure out their days in pupils' tasks' in order to control what is going on in classrooms. Pupils, however, according to Doyle (1986) work hard to avoid difficult and risky tasks by engaging in 'bidding down' such tasks to make them more manageable and safe. The children in this tale were divided in their views of the value of students' activities, influenced by the ethos of the school, by parents' attitudes and by their own previous experience. What their comments do seem to demonstrate, however, are their abilities to judge tasks and activities presented to them. Children obviously do have opinions about the quality of teaching and perhaps we should encourage them to take part in more evaluation activities and empower them within the school–university partnership!

Tutors

Pupils' perceptions of visiting tutors is indicative of their ability to spot an assessment situation. Their hostile reaction to the tutor in this tale may be surprising to those in higher education who see themselves in a more positive light. Such hostile reactions perhaps highlight the need for better communication between adults and children, as to what is happening when the tutor visits. TV addicts of the cult programme *All Quiet on the Preston Front* (Firth 1993) will have seen one of the best examples available, visually, of 'tutor in action'. It occurs when Eric, dressed as a dragon, capable of breathing real smoke, has been recruited by his girl friend to add excitement to her lesson and to impress her tutor. The children assault the dragon, press his 'fire' button which sets off the smoke alarm which brings the fire brigade. In short order the rest of the school is outside the classroom which is now in disarray. The tutor sits impassively writing in his notebook. Observing in classrooms is a delicate activity and needs careful negotiation and sensitive approaches. We discuss elsewhere the need to monitor how many people are observing and debriefing the student illustrated in this tale by the experience of David Brown (see also Chapter 6, 'Triumph and disaster'). Perhaps, though, we also need to consider more the effects on children, the disruption to their routine, and not least how not just students but tutors are to be introduced to the children and gain entry to the classroom, particularly now that their visits are less frequent.

FURTHER READING

Brown, S. and McIntyre, D. (1993) *Making Sense of Teaching*. Milton Keynes: Open University Press. Chapter 2 – Identifying Good Teaching – provides pupils' perceptions of good teaching , through both written and oral comments which elaborate some of the points made by the children in this story.

For a brief discussion of student teachers and their impact on pupils, see Carney, S. and Hagger, H. (1996) 'Working with beginning teachers: the impact on schools', in McIntyre, D. and Hagger, H. (eds) *Mentors in Schools: Developing the Profession of Teaching*. London: David Fulton Publishers.

For a fuller discussion of how pupils perceive classrooms, see Schunk, D. H. and Meece, J. L. (1992) *Student Perceptions in the Classroom*. Hillsdale NJ: Lawrence Erlbaum Associates.

Chapter 6 in Furlong, J. and Maynard, T. (1995) *Mentoring Student Teachers: The Growth of Professional Knowledge*, London: Routledge, contains good descriptions of student teachers trying to establish themselves in classrooms and also deals with humour and 'personal' issues.

Observing students and giving feedback, see Maynard, T. (ed.) (1997) *An Introduction to Primary Mentoring*, London: Cassell, which gives a sensitive approach to observing in classrooms and leads on to discuss collaborative teaching, a sort of participant observer role which may be one of the ways tutors can negotiate a role for themselves in primary classrooms.

To explore the affective domain and issues to do with aesthetic, intuitive and expressive teaching see Woods, P. and Jeffrey, B. (1996) *Teachable Moments: The Art of Teaching in Primary Schools* and Fullan, M. and Hargeaves, A. (1992) *What's Worth Fighting For in Your School?*, both Milton Keynes: Open University Press.

CHAPTER 6

De-briefing: triumph and disaster

It was the day of the Moan Session. Naturally that is not its official title. Its official title is Group De-briefing and Evaluation, and it is when we meet the students from our particular cluster fresh back from their partnership experiences. The link tutor convenes and chairs the session. No other tutor or mentor is present. It fulfils an important role in the way we key university managers – as we like to think of ourselves – appraise the working of partnership and school-based training in primary education. It allows us to gauge how effectively we are meeting our objectives, to ascertain which wrinkles need to be ironed out and then to re-visit our targets for establishing partnership in the next year. It also provides us with a formidable agenda to take to our mentor development meetings when we meet in clusters. Like I say, it's a Moan Session.

Not everything is a complaint but it often seems like that. I am constantly amazed at the way some students view tutors whom I respect, and mentors whom I admire. Not infrequently I am driven by the evidence to revise my opinions. I have a cluster of eight schools, five or six of which usually take two students each for any particular school experience. In this case it was six. That day there was a good attendance and when I opened proceedings there was nearly a full house: eleven of the twelve, two of whom were unfamiliar to me, but I had expected that for reasons I will explain. Peter was ill which was a pity because I knew he'd had a good time and he always contributed positively. I'd hardly begun the warm-up act when two more students came in. These two I also did not know, which caused me some passing confusion. As I said and promised to explain, I knew that there should be two there in the room whom I didn't know, which was right, but now there were four. It meant that two of the students were in the wrong cluster group, or more precisely the wrong room. Since this was the third such meeting I wondered at the impact previous sessions must have had on them. After some confusion we established that two of those present and assembled had been at Thames Road school. I personally do not do the rivers. I knew that Chris did the rivers – always had done. The rivers wove their way through an enormous post-war council development to the north of the city and when fully stocked generated sufficient children for no fewer than six primary schools. They were named after a variety of rivers. When one called out to a colleague in the carpark that one was off to the Nile it simply meant that one was visiting that part of the estate through which flowed the Nile and in which therefore was to be found Nile Place school. I have no wish to labour the point or to give extended details of why four other schools happened to be called – in a mixture of idiosyncrasy and serendipity – Mersey Square, Amazon Lane, Colorado Road and Elbo Street (it's in Spain). I am developing this theme at length for no reason other than to explain how I was able immediately to figure out how these two students, if they had been at Thames Road, should have been with Chris.

'You're with Chris,' I laughed, 'two doors down.' It all added to my carefully developed front as the Omniscient One. 'I knew you weren't with me.'

'I wish we were with you,' one of them called out, reluctant to leave without getting a moan in. After all, that's what they'd come for. 'Chris can be an absolute prat.'

'Don't be unprofessional,' I responded, but secretly I was pleased. Chris *is* a prat. I, of course, am not. There is a further point to the aside about strange faces, which I will come to, but for now I must capture the ambience of that occasion. Thinking back it was a moan session *par excellence*. Within minutes the floodgates had opened.

'My mentor didn't have any time to spend with me – she was always chasing around other staff. In any case, she didn't seem to want me to take her class. She was reluctant to leave me with them. It had a really bad effect on the children. They wrote notes to her on the blackboard – "Dear Mrs Fitzpatrick, PLEASE come back, we miss you and PLEASE don't leave us with Mr Chandler. We don't like him as much as you." She gave me no chance to get to know the children, and it's hardly boosted my morale.'

A second voice followed swiftly on.

'My school wasn't interested in Partnership. In fact when I asked in the staffroom when they had first come into partnership with the university they all looked at me as if I was from a different planet! I half expected to be taken aside by the men in black. "Come in Kevin. We are receiving you."'

The refrain was now being taken up increasingly.

'I'm certain my mentor didn't want me there. I can tell, you know. She said things like, "Never mind children, Mr Harper won't be here tomorrow and we can get on uninterrupted . . . " in a loud voice to the class, and she spelled out "un-in-ter-rup-ted" like it was a word of five syllables.'

I would have communicated my own agreement with the syllable count but another voice was already on air.

'My flatmate walked out of her school after two days. The nursery nurse kept telling her to wash up the paints, cut up the paper, and make sure the toilets were all flushed! She had to go back though. The course leader made her apologise and she had to write a special assignment on how to deal with difficult situations in school. Personally, walking out seems to be a pretty good solution to me. Actually my school wasn't like that at all. It was brilliant.'

I winced. This was awful. I recognised immediately that two of the students were at the same school. I thought I knew who the mentors were and how they got to be mentors. The third student, Kevin in fact, was, in my view, a tricky customer in the first place, to whom trouble happened rather too often. I doubted the total veracity of his story. I set aside a generous pinch of salt but for the moment I was anxious to build on the one positive note which had crept in at the end.

'I'm glad your school was brilliant, Jayne. Tell us about it.'

'It was really great: friendly and supportive. Everyone was prepared to give me the freedom to have a go at things I was interested in. It was a really happy place and I had a dream mentor. She made everything make sense, like all the bits of a jigsaw coming together.'

Jayne's co-placement student Ellie joined in, 'Yes, our placement was ace. I'd recommend it to anyone. I wish I could get a job there. The Head is fully involved. I've learned a tremendous amount. Every day was a brilliant learning experience. I've got a continuous commentary on my experiences and my file is crammed with activities. I really felt part of the team at the school.'

Quickly, a modest chorus of support built up. William – known locally as Bill the Barrack Room Lawyer – somewhat to my surprise, was ready to contribute his own good experience.

'Ours was OK too. The school was very welcoming. They really went out of their way to accommodate us and discussed everything about the placement. I did lots of joint planning. The mentor was everything I would have wanted . . . very helpful and allowed me to try things out. If anything she was over-patient with us. The best thing was that the mentor did not expect me to do things as she did them. She let me experiment and then helped me to evaluate what worked well and what didn't. She's been very helpful, has written lots of comments and observations and made plenty of suggestions.'

I wondered if I might have misjudged William. He was coming across in a more positive light than any time I'd talked to him before in this or any other setting. I reckoned he was growing up.

'Mind you,' he said 'I don't know why we have to do school term dates. It cocks up the term and we have to come back to Uni before all the other students, which costs £40 more and we have to sort out our own food while being on block school experience which you don't feel like doing after a hard day in school. I'm over a hundred quid down.'

William was back on form.

'Thanks William. It's a problem we're familiar with, but we don't seem to make much headway with the wardens who run the halls of residence. They don't seem to be able to adjust to the peculiarities of teacher-training.' I have to confess that my response sounded a little weak.

William – who was now deeply into Bill mode – glowered. 'Pathetic,' he said, 'and there's another thing – not me, but my girlfriend, Tina.'

He was by now fully launched.

'I think we should be able to wear what we like to school. Why should she have to take her nose ring out? The Head said she did not expect to see her and her mate wearing jeans. When she complained to her tutor about not having enough money to buy any more clothes, her tutor said there was a perfectly good Oxfam shop along the road, where she could get kitted out for less than a fiver. That's what she'd had to do when she was a student! That must have been before the flood. My Tina wouldn't be seen dead in an Oxfam shop.'

'I'm not sure I agree with you, William,' I demurred. 'After all, we do have to maintain professional standards and expectations.'

'Standards and expectations!' – a snort – 'How's this for standards and expectations then? Tina's mate – no names, but you know who I mean – she's having to put in a claim for reimbursement for all the "special shampoo" she's had to buy. Ask her how many times she had nits on this placement. It wouldn't have been so bad if she hadn't infected everybody in the house. Her boyfriend moved out – dumped her until after the placement had finished. He couldn't stand the nits. When she told her tutor the tutor just laughed and said, "You can chalk this up to experience", and wouldn't let her come out of the school. That's a real, miserable, unhelpful, couldn't-care-less attitude to student problems, don't you think? Some tutors can be real miseries, and worse.'

Actually, it hadn't been her tutor, it had been me, as the overall Placements Officer. There was a substantial point beneath the grouse. The woman in question had had to pay out £12 for shampoo which was a real hole in her pocket. In the event, we'd fiddled it on the petty cash and got it back for her, which seemed a better practical solution than re-negotiating the placement. In any case, I couldn't begin to think how I would have explained moving her out of the school.

'Excuse me, your kids have got nits, the student's got nits, maybe the staff have got nits, the tutor's scared she'll get nits, so we're off to the leafy suburbs. Why are you scratching your head?' I shuddered.

I raided the petty cash instead. Chicken-hearted but essentially practical – that's me.

'I think I'd like to return to our agenda,' I said. 'So, what was your mentor like?' The question was directed at Jo.

'She was a fantastic mentor, brilliant. She helped me in every possible way. She's got a good sense of humour. We both laughed when we made fools of ourselves. She gave me advice, helped me plan and also sat back and let me find out for myself. She was supportive, challenging but not pushing too fast, like some you know. She was encouraging, did press on key issues and evaluations and tried to get me to develop week by week. She was good at observing lessons, reading my file and talking about issues. She always gave me a written report and oral feedback and helped me analyse the key features of my teaching and then we would agree a focus for the future.'

'That's good,' I said, 'very good' – meaning it. 'Jack?'

'OK me then. Not so sure about the mentor, Shellie. She didn't seem to want to know about the competences. She gave me all her plans and – it was a bit awkward actually as my uni tutor commented on them thinking they were mine! He didn't think much of them. I had to hide his comments from my mentor. To be honest the tutor pushed me a lot harder than Shellie. He wanted more all the time. At first, it seemed like he was pushing me in at the deep end and I felt I needed more time. Then it clicked and it all seemed to come together. My tutor really was excellent. He always had plenty of time for discussion on each visit, met with me and the mentor, answered a lot of our questions about the file and about planning. Best of all, he went through the competences with me and related her comments to them. I got more out of his three visits than all the rest of the advice in the school. I couldn't complain, I suppose, except I wish the mentor had been a lot more demanding. I needed it.'

'It's good when the mentor is really keen and interested.' This from Elaine who had been sitting quietly – which she does a lot. 'But sometimes it can go over the top. My mentor was so efficient I couldn't keep up with all the comments in my file. She used to take it into the staffroom for at least an hour every day and then she'd go through it with a fine toothcomb, and she expected me to write back on every comment. She didn't seem to have a sense of humour and when I made jokey comments in my file she underlined them in red and wrote, "What do you mean by this?" next to it!'

'I was in school with Elaine.' This was Geoff. 'It wasn't just Elaine's mentor. In that school everybody had been trained as a mentor and you couldn't move for advice. It got so bad I complained to my Uni tutor. One day there were three people observing me in class, the classteacher, the mentor and a new member of staff training to be a mentor. I felt like a monkey in a zoo!'

'I think what you've had is better', said William, returning to the fray, 'than what I had on my first school placement.' The strain of being positive was clearly beginning to tell on William. He wanted to be the bearer of bad news so he was into retrospectives. 'The mentor I had then seemed totally indifferent to me, no criticism, no positive comments. Whenever I'd got the class, she went out of the room. She'd had quite a few days off as well. She'd just pop her head round the door and coo "Everything OK?" and then disappear. In the event I was expected to do 15 or 16 lesson plans every week and I was left alone for hours in class to get on with it. Other students were only doing five or six a week.' He couldn't resist that final crack about comparative workloads.

I turned back to the pair who had opened up the discussion with such negative and destructive comments. I was secretly relieved that, as we'd gone on, things had taken a turn for the better and on the whole, thus far on the evidence of this group, I was feeling that school-based teacher-training had a lot going for it. I was feeling sufficiently comfortable in fact to be able to revisit the grumbling discontent of the opening five minutes. As I indicated, I didn't have too high opinion of the two students in question – two men who, with bad luck, might stumble on in a pedestrian way through forty years of service. Alas, we had to keep up the level of our performance indicators and the TTA had enjoined us to win more men for primary schools. I couldn't help thinking that in appearance they looked a bit like the Two Ronnies, except that they were never funny. Quite often they were miserable. It was Ronnie Corbett who spoke up first.

'I don't think our school should have been chosen for a placement. They had a terrible OFSTED, so I told them I didn't think they should have been used. All merry hell was let loose then! Had the tutor in a blue fit! I don't see why we should pussyfoot around – if it's a crap school then we should say so. After that I spent the day with the Head and the tutor trying to smooth things out. In the end I asked that they move me to another school. They wouldn't. The tutor said I had to finish the work I'd started with the class and the Head said he didn't think there was another school good enough. Sarcastic sod.'

Suddenly Kevin was in again, 'Don't you get pigsick of OFSTED? When my school finally worked out who I was they gave me the OFSTED routine. They explained they wouldn't have much time for me because of OFSTED. It seemed to take over everything! If you couldn't do something it was because of OFSTED. If you did something badly they said I'd have to do better when OFSTED came. In the end they decided the mentor should take back her class in OFSTED week. I'm surprised they let me stay in the school. I think they would have preferred to lock me in the cupboard or send me off with the rubbish to the tip.'

I thought, 'I can see their point of view,' but what I said was 'OFSTED is a very trying time for schools. What did you actually do?'

'They said I could observe so I got a clipboard and went into classes who didn't know me. They thought I was from OFSTED.'

'More salt,' I thought, 'more salt, Kevin.'

Ronnie Barker had been waiting patiently to offer his thoughts. His had been the early contribution about the five-syllable experience. He had some more to say about his unwelcoming mentor but it transpired that in fact he had got to teach quite a lot of lessons and, not only that, but his real grouse was not with his mentor but with his tutor.

'When my tutor came in, that day, I was gutted. My tutor observed me and I thought I did a good lesson. Then she tore it apart . . . ignored what she'd observed and moved on to talk about all sorts. She might have praised me. You do it to the kids, don't you. Students need praise too. She didn't mention competences at all . . . says she doesn't understand them and they're being changed anyway. How can you get schools to work with you on competences when snidey tutors keep taking the mickey? All through I felt my tutor had a very negative approach. I wasn't allowed to write that anything had gone well. She only seemed to want to know what went wrong. I've spent a small lifetime having to listen to weekly waffle in college sessions about valuing children and being positive and then I end up with a Uni tutor who only wants negatives. It just about sums up this course . . . wander about and if you are lucky you get a tutor who suits you.'

'Well thank you, the Two Ronnies', I muttered to myself, and I looked at Ronnie Barker in particular and I thought, 'You'll have to do a lot of wandering, my son. I wish you'd wander off for good.' But I said nothing of the sort. What I said was, 'Perhaps we can discuss those problems privately.'

'OK,' he said. 'Why not?'

I love it when the students care passionately about something.

I quickly began to tot up the score. We'd started with the Two Ronnies, Messrs Chandler and Harper, aided and abetted by Kevin, but softened by Jayne whose friend had walked out although she herself had had a great time. We'd heard a lot from William on his own behalf plus the experiences of Tina and Tina's mate who were now doubtless pouring out their troubles in a nearby room. Jo, Jack and Elaine and Geoff had all chipped in, so that left just two silent voices.

These were the two with whom I was unfamiliar. The explanation is complicated and boring. Basically there are eight schools to a cluster but they don't always all have students at the same time. This time only five of mine had been scheduled to be in operation, but because of long term staff absence we had had to disperse one of the clusters. The two students in question had been added to my cluster and allocated to Jemima Johnston Primary School which had very kindly taken them surplus to their agreed commitment for this very important placement, albeit it had meant a fair bit of juggling around at the school. That's the simple part of the explanation. I'd had to communicate to them in writing mainly because at the time it all happened I was myself off to Stockholm to sort out a mess which had arisen with our Erasmus scheme. When I got back, Trisha had been standing in for me with the link visits. I'd gyrated around as best I could but there was no chance of getting to everyone, so using my judgement I had bypassed Jemima Johnston. Why J J? If I'm honest I think it was because I knew the two mentors were Tom and Mark. I have explained that Tom is best taken in small doses. While I was still very cross with Mark I did recognise his qualities as a mentor. After the shock of Sharon, I was sure that Mark would do a good job. Tom I feared would do a Tom job.

'You must be Beverley and Katie?' I said and they nodded.

'You've been at Jemima Johnston?' More nods. 'That's a school I know very well. Let me guess how it went. I think you had a good placement and the Head, the staff and the mentors were very supportive and helpful.'

'Yes.'

'No.'

I digested the collapse of my confident prediction.

'Let's start with the good news. Katie, you voted a resounding, 'Yes'. Tell us about it.'

'I'd echo what several of the others have said. I had a brilliant mentor and he couldn't have been more helpful. He helped me in loads of ways – practical ways – he was always ready to talk and listen and he bailed me out of a couple of difficult situations. His comments were always constructive and in the end he sorted out my PCS for me.'

PCS stands for Personal Curriculum Study. It is part of the honours component to the degree. It is normally a small-scale investigation in the student's specialist subject. The aim of it is to improve practice through locating the study in current initiatives in that subject whilst at the same time making connections to research literature in the field. Normally a student would select about six pupils to focus on and would work with them intensively over ten weeks or so. Students then go back to the school to do the investigating work but it's important that they shape the project and lay the groundwork before they leave. Katie who had showed herself to be a satisfactory to good student who worried a lot, seemed to be well on track. My feelings towards Mark began to soften.

I turned to Bev. I could almost guess what she was going to say.

'I didn't like my mentor at all. He really seemed to have it in for me. He didn't like my planning; he didn't like my file, he didn't like the way I taught; he didn't like the way I marked the children's work. He said my evaluations were no good. He didn't put it as crudely as that but that's what it boiled down to. All in all, he didn't like the way I did things at all and he was always suggesting a different way of doing things. I thought mentors were supposed to help you do your own thing, not always insist that you do it the way they would do it. I took my PCS proposal to him and he tore it to pieces.'

'Why wasn't I there?' I berated myself, and cursed that I had been stuck in Stockholm, tangled up in the usual Euro-botch. 'Let's try to sort out these two experiences,' I suggested.

I have to say that Bev was a student about whom I had had serious reservations. She was one of those people who tumble from disaster to disaster and it's always someone else's fault. Tutors mislead her, college classes mysteriously cancel themselves, buses break down deliberately, work goes missing, phone calls aren't logged and all manner of viruses afflict her. She is more than a bit of a pain. But this time I was sure there was at least a grain of truth in her complaints. Tom had claimed another victim.

'Shall we talk this through as a group? It could be a useful case study and, as you may know, I didn't get round to see Bev and Katie personally because I was in Stockholm, so I would like to discuss it briefly, particularly since it's a school I reckon to know really well. Do you mind?' The group nodded assent.

I could see the rest of the students were intrigued by this talk of diverse experiences in the same school; not only that but the self-same school about which their distinguished group leader was a world expert, self-proclaimed.

'Sounds like good a punch-up,' said Kevin.

'Carry on by all means,' said William 'but remember we have standards and expectations. No tittle-tattle. When we've done, we'll want sound perceptive contextual analysis from you to help us consider the issues.'

I glared and filed him away for future reference.

'Katie, you were happy, you begin.'

Katie, more formally Kathryn, was an ex-nursery nurse, a mature entrant to the BEd course. She was a solid, reliable student, not as assertive as she might be and a little prone to sycophancy with regard to her tutors and mentors in school. She was very much a 'don't rock the boat' type of person. She still lived at home with her elderly parents who relied very much on her, even though she was 26 and solvent. She enjoyed the security of living at home and still had the same friends that she'd always had since leaving school. In fact her life was little different from three years ago or so when she had joined the course. She had spent four years as a nursery nurse in a large nursery school and was much more at home in the early years. She was a victim of the cluster re-shuffle – and it had not been possible for her to have an early years placement at Jemima Johnston Primary School as Meg, the Head of Early Years, had declared that after the last student, Barbara – I won't trouble you with the details – she was giving her department a well-earned rest from students! As a result of this Katie had ended up with Year 4 and she had tried hard to come to terms with a junior aged class. She had arrived just as the school was joining the LEA Literacy Project; indeed I learnt later that her placement had enabled her teacher to attend the five-day course. Katie's specialist subject was English, so she was very interested in hearing about the course. She had had some lectures at university about the Literacy Project and setting up a literacy hour in class, but she was anxious for any practical 'on the ground' tips. Some of this I knew at the time, some, as I have indicated, I learnt later.

'Tell us first about your project.'

'OK, but I have to confess that it wasn't all my idea. Well, it was my idea but I couldn't have worked it out without help – a lot of help.'

I made a mental note to tell Mark about her comments. It would be a way of re-building bridges between us even though I was a little concerned that he might have given her too much help. Katie continued. The focus for the dissertation was to be the effectiveness of a literacy hour in the classroom she was working in. She – they – would set up two groups: those who would be on the receiving end of the literacy hour and those who would not. They would test all the children with the good, old favourite Burt Reading Test. Once tested the children would be put into the two groups. One of them would work with the 'have nots' and the other, Katie, would work with the 'haves' using all the wonderful phonological awareness materials that had been brought back from the Literacy Project course. After ten weeks they would test them again and then they would have proof of whether the literacy hour worked or not. Katie would have been able to trial all the literacy activities and thereby have learned a lot. Meanwhile, the children hopefully would have progressed more in their reading and they could compare the scores of the two groups. Katie was over the moon. She had been dreading the PCS and she had been afraid that her tutor would think she wasn't very bright. She craved all the help she could get.

I decided not to comment.

'Bev, your turn.'

She was clearly embarrassed. 'My project's the same,' she said.

The room was silent and pins were dropping. 'Had you agreed to do the same?'

'Well, not exactly but Katie had told me what she was doing and I said that that sounded like a good idea and I might try something the same. When I thought about it I couldn't think of any way to improve it so I just carried on and Katie never said that I wasn't to do it. In any case, it wasn't very fair. No one was giving me any help working out my PCS. Katie had a mentor who was doing it all for her and I had no one giving me advice.'

The silence continued. Pins had stopped dropping but knives were coming out to cut the atmosphere. This was classic Bev.

'Did you ask your PCS tutor if what you were going to do was OK?'

'He's never there. I've tried lots of times but he's never there. You can never find anyone at this place.'

'He's always there on a Monday afternoon,' I said, with more confidence than I actually felt. 'That's the idea of having Mondays back in college.'

'I don't come in on a Monday afternoon. I've got a part-time job. It's a difficult journey anyway and I can't afford the bus fare. By the time you put the bus fare to the money I'd be losing I just can't afford it and I need the money.'

I had some sympathy. Many students were in dire straits but . . .

'Did you discuss it with your mentor?'

'Yes, when he would listen.'

'And . . . '

'He rubbished it.'

Every now and then I thought Tom will get it right. Something to do with monkeys, typewriters and Shakespeare.

'How exactly did he rubbish it?'

She fished out her file and passed me the notes that Tom had written.

They read, 'I'm afraid there are problems with this PCS.' He had gone on to elaborate:

'"Small scale" for this project as I understand it from the notes from college means six children.

It's ethically wrong in my view to have "have-nots" and "haves" and to test them.

Parents could legitimately complain if their child was not in the privileged group.

How could you be sure it was the literacy activities that improved the children's reading scores and not any other factors such as normal development/starting points/ability/work done at home?

Pre-test–post test is an unreliable method for this type of mini-research.

The purpose of the enquiry, again as I read it, is for the student to design activities and to monitor and assess children's progress.

The Burt test is out of date and discredited.

You make no mention of the National Curriculum and its assessment

I have some suggestions for improvement:

All children take part in the activities

You design your own literacy activities – open to the whole class – but select your six children – giving reasons for selection.

You profile the reading ability of these children using their Key Stage 1 SATs and their reading assessment from school, and your own assessment procedures, designed to give a detailed picture of each child, e.g. miscue analysis, running record, Neale Analysis of Reading.

You chart the development of individuals over the ten weeks through observation, reading interviews, listening to children read, and reading activities.

Your aim should be to develop your understanding and teaching in literacy and to chart the development of a few children.'

I was impressed. I made a mental note that we should get someone in from the Literacy Project to talk to our students. Relatively brief exposure had certainly worked wonders for Tom. Nevertheless, something was bothering me, but I couldn't put my finger on what it was. Then Katie spoke up.

'Do you agree with that?'

'I do actually. I think it's a very thorough diagnosis and prognosis.'

'So if Bev's project, which was mine first, is rubbish, then mine's rubbish too?'

'Well the general idea's good but it needs the sort of polishing which Tom has given Bev's.'

'Tom?' said Katie questioningly. 'What's Tom got to do with Bev's file?'

'I'm talking about the comments he wrote which I've just read out.'

'Tom didn't write that,' Bev almost shouted. 'Mark wrote that.'

I was clearly looking confused.

'You know, Mark, the young one, the carping know-all I got stuck with as a mentor,' cried Bev indignantly.

'You really know this school like the back of your hand, don't you?' offered William.

The penny had dropped.

Katie had said she had had a great, helpful, supportive mentor. It wasn't Mark, as I had rushed to assume. It was Tom. In practice, he'd done a worksheet job again. He'd given her the answers and she had accepted them unquestioningly. Now I understood everything. Tom was one of those people who once he'd been on a short course became the 'world expert' in his school . . . so he was now a literacy expert, and that is how he had come to be advising Katie on her PCS. Tom was not however familiar with educational research methodology, believing research to be about proving things and about experiments, like in science where you had control groups and you tested for results. Not for Tom the finer nuances of ethics and confidentiality, of a research methodology which illuminated and illustrated rather than measured, while issues of equality of opportunity arising from social and educational research never entered his head.

To Katie, Tom was a saviour. Beauty was in the eye of the beholder. As for Bev, she had been so locked into her syndrome of self-pity and blame-transfer, that she had failed to recognise that she had been allocated to an excellent mentor operating at a very high level. Mark's only error – if error it was – seemed to be that he had made the mistake of taking Bev seriously.

As for me, I had made the unforgivable error of accepting, without any real question, the two stereotypes offered to me and then transferring them directly on to the two stereotypes I already held in my mind.

What a prat!

COMMENTARY AND MATTERS FOR DISCUSSION

Mentoring: the importance of context

In this tale a relatively small number of students had a wide variety of experiences. This is not unusual and it reminds us that context is, for some, everything.

Students experience a steep learning curve on school experience placements. Teachers are quick to induct them into the realities of primary schools today. Moyles (1995), in her introduction to a book about beginning teaching, stresses that it is also about beginning learning and acknowledges the interlinked nature of professional and personal attributes and their importance to teaching. She maintains that the process of learning to teach is principally related to 'what *you* bring that develops your professional personality in harmony with your own personality'. The possibilities for conflict and disagreement are numerous, and student dissatisfaction is often high. The importance of hitting it off with one's mentor is crucial to a good experience and there is often a high correlation between doing well and getting on with the mentor. Similarly, the atmosphere in the school and the welcome received by students, as illustrated by Jayne and Ellie's experiences in this tale, set the tone for the placement. Suschitzky and Garner (1995) discuss how important it is that both mentor and student appreciate the complexity of learning to teach and the importance of having a good working relationship, in order to maximise the learning opportunities. Strategies which they suggest involve students in taking joint responsibility for the development of the relationship by avoiding conflict and stressing the positive aspects of their mentor's support. One would hope that such a stance would not affect the students' ability to appraise critically the context of the school and the evaluation of practice in the school. Students experience great pressure to 'fit in' with school norms, especially since the advent of the National Curriculum and the detailed school planning which most schools now engage in. In practice, these pressures reduce the negotiation of what can be taught and limit the opportunities for students to teach across the whole curriculum. Edwards (1997) writes about how the fact that students are seen as guests in the primary classroom does not help their learning. Politeness gets in the way. How schools and mentors encourage a climate where support and challenge both feature has been discussed earlier. The discussion on the role of the higher education tutor, in the commentary in Chapter 8, 'Partners: stormy weather', could have relevance here.

What makes a good mentor? The student view

Within the variety of contexts, this group of students encountered a variety of mentors. Some were 'brilliant'. What makes a mentor 'brilliant', or simply good and effective? Shaw (1992) discusses, in detail, the generic skills of mentoring which cover:

- working with others
- needs analysis
- counselling, negotiation and conflict solving
- giving and receiving positive and negative feedback
- observation and assessment skills
- report writing and
- setting targets.

Students consulted in the Mentoring in Schools project would offer the following as desirable qualities. A good mentor should be:

- clear about his or her role
- experienced in teaching
- able to manage adults
- able to challenge assertively but professionally
- proactive
- able to listen carefully
- able to accept different teaching approaches
- open-minded
- approachable and accessible to staff and students
- trustworthy and able to respect confidentiality
- a role model of good practice
- able to observe teaching and give feedback
- able to remain slightly detached from any situation
- objective whenever possible
- willing to share ideas and talk.

Additionally, a mentor needs to have counselling skills and a sense of humour.

The overall picture of a mentor which emerges is of someone who at one and the same time wears the 'expert teacher' mantle and has the interpersonal skills required of the effective manager of adults. Being a good teacher does not necessarily mean being a good mentor, but it helps. The role model argument is very persuasive.

Making mentoring work

Booth (1993) in reporting on a research project investigating students' views of mentors, matched student confidence in teaching and managing the class with regular and detailed discussion with a mentor. This notion is prominent in our tales, especially this one. Nonetheless, there are necessary conditions. Time for worthwhile discussion was seen as an important factor, in the students' views. It was the issue that one of the Two Ronnies plunged right into. It opened up the main session. It is one of the issues which causes much comparison between students when they talk about their schools. Student experience can also vary within a school, highlighting the very personal nature of mentoring, and the need for a school policy and some, if not perfect, clarity as to the role of a mentor. Booth (1993) also found that students valued mentors who treated them like professionals and who adopted a not too directive style of counselling. Edwards and Collison (1996) expressed major concerns about how students can often not be recognised as learners in school, being made to feel that they are 'real teachers' and therefore should become an 'extra pair of hands' in a busy primary classroom. (For a discussion of this issue and that of 'legitimate peripheral participation' refer back to the tale about Mike – and its commentary). Booth states that the findings of his small-scale research project indicate that 'in the early stages of their work in schools, students are principally looking for support which is positive, unthreatening and readily available'.

This ties in with what has been discussed about stages of development in learning to teach and the early stage of 'personal survival', Furlong and Maynard (1995). (See again the commentary on Mike's tale in Chapter 3 for further discussion.) But do students seek or desire a mentor who is only going to be positive? Does the evidence supporting the claim that mentors lack the capacity to challenge need to be modified to take into account students' need to be supported rather than challenged? The work of Furlong and Maynard (1995) and McIntyre (1992) would lead us to expect students in the 'moving on stage', or at McIntyre's third 'critical level' to be acknowledging the need for challenge, perhaps actively seeking challenge or at least being able to cope with mentors who do challenge them. Jayne and Ellie were appropriately challenged. William experienced a different sort of challenge. Kevin couldn't handle challenge. Geoff found challenge overfacing. The Two Ronnies were incapable of recognising challenge, but the area of real confusion lay in the experiences of Katie and Bev. Both were confused about challenge, seeing it differentially as support and criticism.

Power relationships

To greater or lesser degree, all the students were in some form of power relationship with their mentors.

Issues of power in relation to students and mentors cannot be ignored. McIntyre and Hagger (1993) warn of distinctive dangers with regard to assessment: 'The concentration into the hands of one person of the power to guide and assess the development of an individual learner-teacher's practice brings obvious dangers of *arbitrariness and idiosyncracy*' (our italics).

This could mean that personal feelings about the student would influence decisions about competence, always a difficult situation which many university tutors know well. Students always want to do well and many put undue pressure on their mentors to give them higher grades and positive feedback. Some students experience teacher jealousy when they make good relationships with children which can result in teachers guarding their children and classrooms and finding it difficult to let go and allow students to demonstrate what they can actually do. Both Ronnies had that experience. Overzealousness in a mentor is also difficult for students to deal with, as evidenced by Elaine's remarks about how efficient her mentor was in commenting in the file and by Geoff's 'feeling like a monkey in a zoo!'

Guarding against arbitrariness, idiosyncracy and inconsistency is a major headache for those charged with the responsibility of Quality Assurance, traditionally seen as the domain of higher education (Glenny and Hickling, 1995). But in a partnership model of teacher education, is that view right? Bines and Welton (1995) suggest strategies to encourage more teacher participation in Quality Assurance procedures. These include 'teachers in partner schools visiting each other . . . watching different students at work'. They also include tutors working in schools and teachers working in universities. The permutations are many and various. What matters is the wish or will to share the responsibility.

The OFSTED factor

Kevin was 'pigsick' of OFSTED. He should be so lucky! He could walk away. OFSTED's presence is to be felt in several of the tales and the impact of an OFSTED inspection on a school's willingness to accommodate students is increasingly becoming a major issue. Any fairminded person can appreciate the reasons why a school would decide to renege on a previous agreement to take students. Such reasons would include overload of work on teachers leading up to the inspection, not knowing the quality of students allocated, which could affect teaching grades, and more altruistic feelings that the students would not get a fair deal because of work overload. Whatever the reasons, OFSTED does cause problems for universities trying to organise placements for students. Arguably, the inclusion of a criterion in the inspection framework, about the school's role in the training of teachers might help this situation. Another OFSTED issue is the one raised by Ronnie Corbett in this tale – the school which has not had a satisfactory OFSTED report. Officially, universities are normally expected not to place students in 'at risk' or failing schools, or schools with 'special measures'. The result could be that such schools may feel ostracised. There may be good reasons for not using them in terms of requiring students to be exposed to good practice, but such schools can often be helpful and supportive and contain teachers who are, in fact, good role models. Excluding them does little for public relations between schools and universities. Whatever, the spectre of OFSTED remains with us and openness and frank discussion ought to be the order of the day. As students are expected according to the Standards for NQTs (1997) to be able to use and understand OFSTED evidence, we should expect further dialogue among schools, OFSTED and TTA about this issue.

Mentors' knowledge

Mentors' knowledge about the students' course emerged as a parallel issue in the story.

Tom got Katie into a mess partly because he didn't know enough about her course, partly because he didn't understand research methodology and partly because he didn't know enough about literacy. He lacked specific knowledge, specialised knowledge and subject knowledge. Mark had these qualities. Do mentors need 'subject knowledge'? How can they remedy deficiencies in students' 'subject knowledge'? The issue was introduced in Paula's tale and discussed more fully in relation to Mike – but that was in the context of students' personal subject knowledge.

Mentoring subject knowledge in primary schools raises particular problems, discussed by Maynard (1996) and Edwards and Collison (1996). Not the least is the extent of mentors' own subject knowledge and their ability to challenge and develop students in this area. Maynard identified 'profound difficulties and tensions in teachers' beliefs and attitudes', with teachers preferring child-centred approaches rather than subject centred.

Mentoring subject knowledge in the primary school is the focus of Maynard's (1996) chapter in McIntyre and Hagger's book, which came out of the National Project and the Swansea-based element. She describes a project based at Swansea whereby mentors worked with university tutors in planning and supervising student teachers' learning activities. Conclusions indicated that mentors' difficulties with subject knowledge and understanding of substantive content and their understanding of the more theoretical subject principles underlying their activities, appeared to indicate the need for continued involvement of university staff.

Mentors' ability to give appropriate advice on research methods for small-scale enquiries, support students' tasks in the classroom, enhance their subject knowledge as they learn to teach in the classroom, are just a few of the instances which are called to mind. This has implications for the preparation and training of mentors, as courses are revised in the light of Circular 10/97. How can mentors possibly stay familiar with the ever-changing landscape of government/TTA requirements? How can higher education possibly keep them up to date? It is emerging, in another guise at the time of writing, with the challenge to mentors in supporting students in the design of Literacy Hour activities and Numeracy. Sometimes students can seem more informed about new initiatives so that teachers look to them to support their work in Maths and English amid the clamour to make teaching a research-based – or should that be evidence-based – profession. The chance for students to undertake small-scale research in classrooms, as Katie and Bev were doing, is an opportunity for schools in partnership with universities to engage in collaborative research, to benefit from students' research and to learn more about the children and the curriculum. It does however require good communication and cooperation if the Tom situation is to be avoided! Perhaps it is, in any case, too high an expectation – an example of partnerships running before they can walk.

98 *School-Based Teacher Education*

FURTHER READING

Learning to teach and beginning to teach can be further explored in the following texts:

Moyles, J. (ed.) (1995) *Beginning Teaching: Beginning Learning*, Milton Keynes: Open University Press, provides an interesting set of papers spanning classroom contexts, planning for learning, curriculum ideas and working with experienced others.

Woods, P. (1995) *Creative Teachers in Primary Schools*, Milton Keynes: Open University Press, is a refreshing read which focuses on teacher's self and how teachers seek to determine the constitution and expression of self within their own conception of professionalism. Chapter 2 'Resisting through collaboration: a whole school perspective on the National Curriculum' is an account of how one school, through collaboration, resisted the 'strait-jacket of National Curriculum on planning and teaching', which links with the idea of lack of opportunities for students to negotiate their teaching.

Student views of mentoring and mentors are, at this stage, seemingly under-researched but discussion can be located in Booth, M. (1993) School-based training: the students' views', in Booth, M., Furlong, J., Wilkin, M. (eds) (1993) *Partnership in Initial Teacher Training*. London: Cassell.

Also useful for a perspective on how new teachers receive mentoring, see Tickle, L. (1993) The wish of Odysseus? New teachers' receptiveness to mentoring', in McIntyre, D., Hagger, H., Wilkin, M. (eds) (1993) *Mentoring: Perspectives on School-Based Teacher Education*. London: Kogan Page.

For a detailed guide to mentoring, in particular mentoring English and Mathematics, see Maynard, T. (ed) (1997) *An Introduction to Primary Mentoring*. London: Cassell. Part B of this book should be useful for mentors wishing to find activities to help them mentor primary students in English and Maths.

Stephens, P. (1997) 'Student teachers' concerns and accomplishments on main school placements: what school mentors can learn from them', *Mentoring and Tutoring* 5, 1. While being secondary school focused, this article reports on the things school mentors do that student teachers find helpful and unhelpful.

CHAPTER 7

Mentors' stories: Wilma, Tom, Meg and Mark

The letter took me by surprise. Events at Jemima Johnston Primary School had been lively and interesting since we had set off on the partnership road. There had been one or two tricky situations to resolve but now after several years things were settling down. Or so I thought. We had four mentors clearly established with Damien waiting in the wings. Other members of staff were showing interest, but the mentoring duties were being discharged in reasonable rotation by those four. No one's perfect but on the whole I was content with the gang of four. I was comfortable with my role as link tutor within that school in addition to my overall job as Placements Officer. The Head was helpful and supportive. When I went there they were friendly, welcoming and healthily disrespectful. Tom was my unfavourite – hard to work with for all the reasons I've explained elsewhere. After a big hiccup it seemed that Mark had much to offer. I just had to think twice about which student to place with him. Meg and Wilma were great. I was amazed that they were both still at the school. Had they wanted to move, I was sure that they would find suitable promotions. Mark too, I thought. Mentor turnover was always going to be a problem in the new partnerships. We had learnt that from our experience of working with secondary schools, but in this case there was a strong stable situation.

The letter disabused me. Signed by all four, it requested a meeting. They said that they had enjoyed mentoring students but problems had begun to multiply. They referred not so much to the difficult cases and challenging situations they had all become involved in which they saw as special cases. Their main concern was over a number of issues which they wanted to air which made their mentoring tasks so frustrating that they thought they might want to withdraw. Could we talk? We certainly could.

We met at the school, after school, in their attractive little library converted from an old cloakroom. They'd got sponsorship support for it from the local hamburger joint. I mention this only because it gave us a calm, cheerful, unthreatening environment to talk in.

'Don't take fright,' Meg said, 'we're not going to tear you limb from limb, and I don't think any of our problems are the university's fault. I'm not even sure that the university can solve them. We're not going to desert you immediately either; maybe not at all, and all the placements for next term are secure, but we've been comparing notes and a number of issues have arisen which we want to think through. In any case, it's good to talk, isn't it?'

'Have you tried getting sponsorship from BT?' I quipped, but their laughter was polite only. I could see that there were things they were really worried about. 'Why don't you just tell me about the problems?'

Meg seemed to be holding the conch, so she continued.

'A lot of it's stressful,' she said, 'and some of it's getting to us. A key problem is when it's obvious that the student you're working with isn't doing very well. They're probably not going to fail but they're not doing as well as they should. There are two particular difficulties. The first is the feeling of being to blame. You think: "This student is my responsibility. If he isn't developing then it must be my fault." Matching that, and this is the experience of all of us, is that it's precisely the weaker students who are into denial.'

I asked exactly what she meant.

'I mean they think it's our fault, not their fault. When we started the mentoring, you stressed the importance of giving helpful, supportive comment. So we did, but that's all some of them seem to hear or read in our comments. They ignore the rest. I'm fed up saying things like, "It's clear the children like you and you seem to relate well to them as individuals." The good students are hypersensitive to criticism, but someone like Barbara, who lasted four weeks, remember, which was three weeks and four days too long, made me want to scream at her that she was idle, unpunctual, she didn't plan, she didn't collect work, she didn't mark work, she was boring, and she shouted over the noise. I could go on and on. In the end, you will recall, she wrote in saying she wasn't coming back for the last two weeks because although she'd always wanted to teach, she simply wasn't getting any support from us – or you, if it comes to that – and she was upset. Poor dear.'

I tried reason. 'You did the best you could. What's wrong with that?'

'What's wrong is that, although what you say is true, she'll never retrieve the situation and the profession will no doubt be well rid of her, here was someone who ostensibly wanted to be a teacher who was given to me to develop and I couldn't do it. A part of me thinks I failed.'

'When a child does badly in the SATs do you think it's your fault?'

'Sometimes – a bit – but mainly I think I've done the best I can, so I accept it.'

'There's no difference,' I said. 'They raise essentially the same issue – Barbara, Wilma's mad Mike with the whistle and no doubt, somewhere, Fiona the phantom of the future. You did the best you could. In the end it was *their* best, not yours, that wasn't good enough. Take Mike. It was right that he failed. If Wilma had somehow found a way to drag him through, that's what would have been wrong. The odds are he would have blown up in the future, possibly in a situation where he might have done a lot of damage. He wasn't working to his strengths. He needed better career guidance.'

'OK,' said Wilma 'I don't know about Meg but I feel a little better. But that's only one of our troubles. I'm the deputy head, right; that's my day job. Mentoring is something I do partly because I am the Deputy Head, but it's not my only duty. I owe something to the staff. I'm also a class teacher these days and I owe it to my class too, to do the best job I can. I owe it to the parents, some of whom can get very stroppy. There is a duality of roles as mentor to students and teacher of children. This year I am class-based and I only get supply cover when I do the overarching mentoring coordinating role, as opposed to being a class teacher–mentor. There are great pressures in marrying both responsibilities. It feels as if you are pulled in 24 different directions. There is a lot of disruption for children. In addition, other staff miss out on my support because of my involvement in mentoring students. My duties include staff support and development. Mentoring, even with supply cover, takes me away from those staff development duties. The first year we did this I wasn't class-based, but I had a regular timetable releasing other teachers for various things. Oddly, sometimes that made it worse. It's easier to cover for one class teacher rather than have a supply teacher who has to cover some of the eight classes that I take during the week. Moreover, supply teachers create problems of continuity for children and staff. We'd all rather have "internal" rather than "external" supply teachers in the interests of quality support, continuity and coherence for both staff and pupils, but now that staffing levels have had to be reduced – which is why I'm now class-based – we don't have "in-house" supply any more.'

Tom joined in, 'I think a payment should be made to the mentor.'

'That's up to the school,' I said. 'We pass across funding on the basis of supply cover – as agreed when we had those Nuremberg rallies all round the Metropolitan area. What the school does with it is up to the school and it's quite OK by us if the school wants to pay mentors, although we do say that we favour a whole-school approach to mentoring and individual payments seem to run contrary to the spirit of that. We think it's the school's business.'

'Don't agree,' said Tom.

'Neither do I,' said Meg, 'but not for the same reason. I'm dead against additional payments, partly because of what you say, but we have to be careful to show that the whole school gets a fair share of any resource coming in. I don't think the university gives a strong enough lead.'

'It's peanuts anyway,' Mark entered the discussion.

'Peanuts,' I thought. 'You've made me think of nutmeg, which always reminds me of you. Why do I keep thinking bad thoughts about you even though I reckon you are a good guy really?' I smiled wryly, but I didn't reveal my thoughts. Instead, 'You're right though,' I said, 'it is peanuts, though it's more than we can afford. It's crystal clear to everyone involved that school-based training is more expensive than the original model, though no one is putting any resources into it. I wish someone would wake up to the problem.'

'I don't want to talk about money,' said Wilma.

'Nor me,' said Meg.

'I wish I hadn't started it,' and Wilma made a gesture of sweeping it off the table. 'There are more important topics to air.'

'Go on,' I urged.

'Well,' she said, 'I'm not sure we are fully competent. I'm certain we can provide help and support but I suspect there are some things only the university can provide. I actually think, present company excepted, that higher education was doing a decent job before we switched into partnership.'

'Thank you for your qualified support.'

'No, seriously. I agree – we all do – that there should be more time in school for students in initial training. That said, totally, or even predominantly, school-based training is not a realistic or a desirable goal. I have real concerns and anxieties about schools' potential contribution. I'm worried that we might not be able to offer the students important things they need. You have a lot of expertise back at the university. We can help students cope with school but we don't have a background in the literature or philosophy. Teachers I've spoken to generally valued the tutors' contributions when they used to do all the supervision. They could see the wide experience of other schools which tutors had, and most – not all – would acknowledge the high quality training – not just the subject matter, but the thinking processes and analytical techniques which university staff encouraged in their students. More time in school certainly helps students make up their minds more quickly about whether teaching is for them or not, but there's a price to pay. I know there's a stereotypical view of some starry-eyed theory bound tutor, overdosing on "real" books or phenomenology – and some of your lot really are Lulus – but on the whole, I don't want the link between teaching and higher education and research broken.'

'Which is not to say you couldn't cut out some of the jargon,' interjected Tom. 'What on earth is all this contextual analysis?' Eyes rolled behind his back.

'Derek thinks the work some students have done has laid a basis for the school development plan,' said Mark – and I knew to whom he was referring.

'Derek thinks if he can lift chunks out of anywhere it will save him a job,' was Tom's rejoinder. 'Let's get back to this theory lark. Here's an example – I really haven't a clue what you mean when you say you're trying to make a student an anonymous practitioner.' He subsided.

'Autonomous,' I murmured.

'Please, let's be more serious,' said Meg. 'I have a real problem I want to share, and it's to do with loyalty.'

We looked at her and waited for her to go on.

'Some students can be very critical – both of the school and other teachers – and frankly sometimes privately I agree with them. I, too, wonder why some members of staff don't follow the agreed curriculum. I, also, think that our behaviour policy needs revision. I, also, feel that someone, whose name I won't mention, lets the children run riot in the playground and even sometimes turns a blind eye to bullying. I can remember one student, Karen, a young lady of very strong opinions, which she was prepared to air openly, urged changes in the life of the school, and wanted us to change current practice. I felt I had to be loyal to school policy in the staff meetings and this caused me a problem when I was mentoring her. She kept pressing me on whether I agreed because I reckon she knew I did and she wanted me to support change. There have been a number of instances where I have felt compromised. On top of this I found myself struggling sometimes with issues of confidentiality. If people tell you they don't want anything going back to the Head, you have to use your judgement, try to make clear boundaries, about what has to be either left unsaid, remain confidential, or be made known to certain people, for the good of the school. You have to manage the situation. I'm just so uncomfortable with some of it. Then sometimes I find myself worrying about a different sort of loyalty. Are my class being loyal to me? Once I caught myself thinking that they seemed to like the student – Sharon it was – more than me. I tried to persuade myself that it was because she let them get away with more than I would. I told myself she was spoiling the relationship I had with my children. Then I caught myself and I thought, "Meg – that's pathetic." And it was, but it bothered me.'

'Well, I have to say none of this bothers me all that much,' interjected Tom. 'I can't be doing with all the theoretical claptrap, as I've said.'

'You certainly have,' I thought, 'several times'.

'However, what gets me is the waste of scarce classroom resources. Why do they want to use the best art paper all the time? Why do they use only one side of the paper for photocopying? Why can't they learn to sharpen pencils carefully instead of mangling them and why don't they send kids away who don't really want their pencils sharpening, but just want a wander out to the front? Why do they have to triple mount the children's work? I know why,' he continued, 'it's to impress you lot, you tutors, that's why and,' by now he was in full flow, 'why do they use the whole school's store of batteries in the electricity topic? Finally, why don't you tell them about this at college. I know why, it's because you're too busy filling their heads with claptrap about becoming anonymous reflective practitioners, that's why.'

'Autonomous,' I murmured again, but I had decided to say nothing.

'Don't think I don't like having students. Some of them are quite promising and I think they're going to be good teachers. I'll help *them*. The useless ones, well, good riddance, but I just don't think you make our job easy.'

'Tell me more,' I said.

Tom took this as an invitation 'OK, I will. This term I've been lucky. Luckier than Meg was anyway. That Barbara was a right little madam. I don't know how Meg put up with her – I'd have booted her out pronto. By contrast, my Autumn Term student Pat was a "good 'un". I can tell the "good 'uns" very quickly.'

'I'm sure you can,' I smiled at him.

'We talked about the class and she knew to watch where the trouble was likely to come from. I've got them separated out but I wanted her to know in case any of them tried to get back together when I wasn't there. Never mind, I'm not getting to the point.' I marvelled at Tom's self-perception.

'My point is to do with a problem she had when she wasn't working with the whole class. I approve of whole-class teaching, by the way, not all the time but for lots of things. I think it's efficient. It treats everyone as equals and it doesn't half rip through the work. However, I don't do it all the time because I also agree that for some things they need to be in groups. Anyway, Pat's tutor was that Jeremy guy who was at the jamborees – some sort of coordinator. He's been here before and can he talk! I don't mean all the time, like not letting other people get a word in edgeways, though there's certainly something of that about him.'

Tom's diatribe was becoming interminable and I wondered where it was going. I didn't expect any surprises. I didn't get any.

'What I mean about his talk is the words he uses. He never uses one when six will do. He never uses a word of one or two syllables when three or four will do. Anyway, he's drilled it into Pat about being reflective and "open ended" as well as being this anonymous reflective practitioner . . . '

'Autonomous,' I silently sneered at him. Maybe I mumbled aloud a little.

' . . . and he told her that she should concentrate more on differentiation and that she was treating the class too homogeneously. She said that she was just trying things out. He said that wasn't right and at this stage of her professional development she should be concentrating on differentiation because that fitted in with the rhythm of the course. Basically, it was "Do as I say". I don't see how that helps her become autonomous. Did I get your word right? Makes her anonymous I reckon.'

I looked at Tom wondering, just wondering, if he might actually be having a little dig, in a way far more subtle than I had been giving him credit for.

'Anyway,' he continued, 'differentiation is what he wanted, so differentiation was what he got. I gave her some of my worksheets targeted at different ability levels and told her to give them out and let them get on with it. I also told her to pay no attention to Jeremy. It was *my* class. She was with me, I was her mentor and she wasn't to go wandering off into some theoretical jungle. But – and this is my point – I do find it hard to work with some of your tutors. They seem to have a completely different agenda. I've been in teaching now for quite a few years. I know my class, I know my children, I know what I'm doing, I can give your students sensible practical advice and guys like Jeremy just get in the way.'

'I'm sure he doesn't mean to,' I said. 'How about you Mark? You've been very quiet? Do you have any problems?' I reckoned that Mark was going to stay quiet. In fact, I had a hunch that he was finding the session a bit embarrassing.

'On the whole,' said Mark, 'I find mentoring a pretty positive experience. It's like being on a course without actually being on a course, if you see what I mean.'

I did, and the others nodded, including Tom. 'And it refreshes the parts other in-service experiences don't touch.'

I thought to myself that Mark had decided to be very positive, which I figured that he figured was a smart move. Given the situation with Sharon, I thought he was right. But then, I'd never thought he was stupid.

'This might sound funny,' he said, 'but mentoring the students has made me realise quite how much expertise I actually have. It's also enhanced my status or, at least, my image of what I see as my status. It raises me at least a notch as a class teacher. Some parts of the USA call people like us – their sort of mentors – master teachers, don't they?'

'Yes,' I replied, 'and they have to be qualified to be a "master teacher".'

'Do they get paid more?' Tom snapped out.

'I believe they do.'

Happily Mark continued. 'In addition,' he said, 'I've learned a lot from students I've had in all sorts of curriculum areas and in the process I've developed valuable skills through mentoring.'

'Like what?' asked Meg.

'The sorts of things I'm thinking of are interpersonal skills, obviously, but also time management, resource management and people management.' Then he surprised us.

'I also learnt', he said, 'that if you're not careful you can get yourself into a real mess. Let's be frank, I got myself into a mess with Sharon in a particular sort of way but there's an underlying problem in the situation generally. It's to do with how close you get to your mentee. And I don't mean what you're all thinking. I'm talking about things you've all alluded to. What are you? Are you a supporter or are you an assessor? The closer you get the harder it is to fail the student. I'm guessing here because I've never had a failing student, although I've come very close with Bev. I think it must be awful. I find even the routine act of being judgemental very stressful, as they said it could be on the course. I recognise that part of the partnership thrust is so that professionals in the field can be involved more closely in the assessment of students – as a professional act – but in reality I find it hard. On the whole I'd prefer it if you' – he turned to me – 'were doing that bit and I was doing the advising, counselling and supporting. I can see how that looks to be chickening out, but if those were the rules of the game, I'd feel a lot more comfortable.'

We talked this through for quite a while longer. The others were prepared to go further than Mark in accepting responsibility for assessment – Tom was prepared to go all the way – but they clearly shared some of his reservations.

'One last thing from me,' said Mark. 'When you place students with mentors, I think you should give a lot more thought to issues of age difference and gender difference.'

There was an uncomfortable silence. I knew exactly what he meant about gender. Age I wasn't so sure about, but it set me thinking about the concept of 'hidden mentors'. How often is it that whatever the official structure, many young students turn to relatively inexperienced 'other' teachers, often NQTs, with whom to share their problems? At the same time, I remembered how uncomfortable the relationships had been between some mature students and their younger mentors.

Mark was not really bothered about the age gap. For him this was his chance to exorcise the ghost of his relationship with Sharon. He plunged on, remarkably thoughtfully, and raising issues which I recognised transcended his own experience and were not specific to that.

'A man mentoring a woman sees things from a different perspective. If men only ever mentor men, they may not be in situations which help them understand a woman's point of view, and vice versa. Women wouldn't understand the emotional pressures some men suffer from, such as negative self-image.'

I began to recognise that young Mark had quite a problem here, and his comments became increasingly revealing.

'Mentoring is about communication, and men and women have to make an effort if they are truly to relate by trying to use a common language. Men are socialised at an early age into not sharing or talking about their feelings. They are simply not used to talking at this level and it has repercussions. Maybe women are better equipped to be mentors. Gender relationships involve control and power and both men and women can manipulate the mentoring process. Men can feel threatened by some women, while men can also dominate relationships, and could harass women. I might show more gentleness to a woman who was struggling, than I would to a man who was struggling – I might tell the man to pull himself together or something like that. If I was mentoring a male teacher, it would change my behaviour and language.'

Meg joined in and there was some tension in the air.

'Gender *is* an issue in mentoring. It can either be ignored or thought about in constructive ways. I think that basic and fundamental to the process of mentoring is the participants' ability to behave professionally.'

'Ouch,' I thought, 'she's going to put the boot in.' In the event she held off. She even sounded bookish. I sensed that she was holding back strong feelings.

'Mentoring is not a power game but it has the potential to be explored as such. Gender as a factor affecting relationships in mentoring is much more of an issue in longer-term mentoring, e.g. mentoring an NQT for a year in school. It's easy to stereotype expectations. To be of use, mixed gender pairings need to have time to spend discussing expectations, before the mentor–mentee relationship is organised. Personal preference, or being allowed to choose your mentor, needs to be considered in schools.'

We were struggling with the complexities of this issue until Tom decided to join in. 'I think it's good to have a mix. Each can help the other. For example, I think the issue most affected by gender is discipline. Most women students, most women too in my view, are a bit soft on discipline. Also I think men can help students a lot when it comes to the curriculum, particularly in science and technology. On the other hand, speaking personally you understand, I'm always glad to have young women come in with good ideas on poetry and things "arty". I don't see it as a problem.'

There then followed what can only be described as a lively discussion, during which I sat back, happy that attention had moved away from me. Eventually the argument ground to a halt amid the embarrassment of four hosts neglecting their guest.

I decided to seize the bull by the horns. 'Why exactly did you ask me to come? You've said you aren't going to dump us; you've said there are problems. In the main the problems seem to be coming from unanticipated areas of stress and tension rather than any misconception of the relationship or maladministration on our part. Where do you think we are going?'

'There is a problem,' said Wilma, 'and, by and large it's your problem. You have here four mentors who've been doing the new style job of "having students" for several years. Frankly, that may well be enough at the level of intensity at which we've been working. We need some fresh blood. Other mentors should be coming up from the rest of the staff. There are a couple showing interest but it's not enough and there seems to me to be no programme or policy from the University to generate more or to put new programmes in place. Beyond that, what about us? We've done the basic mentoring as set out for years now. Is that it? Is that the extent of our involvement? Mentors need developing too and *we* need something to take us on further. Just as good students do. It seems to me that the new school-based training brings good students on very fast, but then what? How do we stretch them?'

'I agree with all that,' Meg joined in 'but apart from that, even if we wanted a lifetime of mentoring, stretching out into a golden future, we might move on. I certainly intend to look for a job as head of my own infant school with a nursery, or as a Deputy Head of a primary school; or do some job in a junior school to gain experience because I want to be a head teacher of a primary school, so I'm looking around.'

'I have two interviews for Headships coming up,' said Wilma. 'It's no secret.'

'I've only been here not quite a couple of years,' said Mark, 'but I intend to move on – or up.'

'You can count on me,' said Tom 'I'm not moving. If the current lot move on, like Wilma, saving her blushes, and there's an internal vacancy, then Barkis is willing, but I actually think that there's something satisfying about giving long service to the same school. I'd actually have liked to be one of the traditional village schoolmasters. You could have sent all the students you want as apprentices. Seriously, though, you can count on me, but I would like a bit of a rest next year.'

'Does Derek know about all this?' I enquired.

'Doubt it,' said Wilma. 'He likes us being a mentoring school; talks about it a lot. He's up to something anyway. He's called this Staff Development Day on school-based training in three weeks, as one of the teacher days. We always have one at the end of year. It's supposed to be "Planning for next year". We get a speaker in the morning and then we tidy out the classrooms and cupboards for the rest of the day.'

'I'm the speaker,' I confessed. 'I'm supposed to be reviewing the progress of Jemima Johnston Primary School, as a mentoring school. Then Derek says he has a little surprise planned.'

Everyone looked at each other in some puzzlement. 'Maybe he's going to say he'll do all the mentoring,' said Mark.

'Maybe not,' said Tom.

It was time to go.

'Don't look so worried,' said Wilma. 'We'll keep you afloat for a bit longer. Maybe I'll get a Headship at a school which isn't in Partnership, so I can make it my first major initiative.'

The meeting broke up. Mark slipped out; Meg stuffed her bag full of a week's work and Tom bid me a cheerful goodbye.

'Keep sending them,' he said, 'and I'll keep turning them into teachers.'

'Don't worry about him,' said Wilma as we walked out, 'his heart's in the right place. But you know what we call him?' she asked.

'No.'

'The Clone Ranger.'

COMMENTARY AND MATTERS FOR DISCUSSION

Mentoring – a new form of Continuing Professional Development (CPD)

Wilma, Meg, Tom and Mark are in their several ways genuinely interested in, and challenged by, the task of mentoring. They also see it as contributing to their own professional development.

Generally it is accepted that 'mentoring is good for you', professionally. What is more difficult to find evidence of, is what kind of professional development is promoted by mentoring students. Some, like McCulloch and Locke (1994), have argued that every teacher can be an effective mentor. Arguably there are teachers who are unsuitable for mentoring because of their lack of appropriate expertise. There are others like Tom, who never seem to change or develop much, but may yet discharge a useful role, up to a point. Some research (Furlong and Maynard (1995), Elliott and Calderhead (1993)), suggests that there is substantial impact on teachers' professional development in a number of areas. It is also important to remind ourselves that some teachers, before they became mentors, had many valuable attributes and skills, and that mentoring simply provided the opportunities to utilise and enhance them. Areas which mentors might well identify as previous strengths would include: counselling colleagues and pupils, listening to concerns, empathy with beginning teachers, target setting, and profiling techniques. Mentors do not arrive at mentoring with a blank sheet of paper. Nonetheless they experience development. Some areas in which it could be argued that mentors experience worthwhile development are discussed below.

Management and interpersonal skills

An impressive set of skills – management, counselling, team-working and communication with adults – can be observed among mentors. These tend to be early skills. The management and resolution of conflict is more usually an area of further development for a significant number of mentors, as, in the promotion of collaboration, they encounter personality clashes and conflicting priorities. Wilma's brushes with Class Next Door are but a tiny example.

Tomlinson (1995) draws upon Egan's work (1990) in developing the 'skilled helper' approach as part of his useful book on mentor preparation and training, which relates to and expands the findings from other research, e.g. Claxton (1989), Dreyfus and Dreyfus (1986) and Holding (1989).

The statements below are examples of comment to be found all over the country.

'My status, self esteem and value have risen.'
'Being a mentor gives you status in school.'
'Contact with tutors had made me feel much more like an equal partner.'
'I'll be able to put this on my CV.'

The growth in the self esteem and status of mentors is encouraging to note, and well overdue in relation to valuing classroom teachers' expertise. The current TTA- and government-supported campaign to recruit teachers to 'sell' the profession and help end the threat of shortage could usefully draw on material unearthed in the development of school-based training.

Conversely, Tomlinson (1995) recognises that mentors can experience dilemmas which will adversely affect their self-esteem, as they grapple with new situations and encounter searching questions from students.

Raising professional awareness

Teachers engaged in mentoring often report that their observational skills have been improved, that they have become more aware of what being a teacher involves, and have learned to consider and articulate professional issues before their own personal feelings. As with Tom, there is great pressure for teachers, in helping students to develop their teaching, to 'clone' them in their own image. Where there is more than one mentor in a school, this aspect could be avoided by building into the observation and judgemental process two points of view. That would be a start, but one hopes professional dialogue would go beyond those directly involved. Mentors claim that, where school-based training takes place, staffroom discussions can become more focused on issues related to teaching and that overall the level and frequency of professional discourse improves, due to the need to provide students with an environment which facilitates development. Mardle (1995: 162), when discussing the consequences of mentoring and the value of autonomous classroom teachers, states, 'Fundamental to this will be the acceptance that mentoring is a vital ingredient that all teachers need to be involved in as they develop their own professional expertise.'

Arguably, too, teachers can heighten their own awareness of professional issues through engaging in work set by the university for students, an instance of how partnerships in CPD might germinate and develop and prosper. An interesting question arising from teachers being more involved in the training of the next generation of teachers is whether teachers who trained in partnership models of courses have a different notion of professionalism to those who did not? Likewise do schools which participate in school-based training evolve different sorts of support models from those which do not? At least as interesting is whether NQTs who enter schools fully involved in mentoring do better than NQTs who enter schools which have not participated in the post-1992 change? At a conference at Keeble College, Oxford in 1995 – the national climax of the Esmée Fairbairn mentoring project – HMI suggested that they were uncovering evidence to suggest the latter suggestion was true. The question has not been systematically pursued.

Developing new ideas and practices

Apart from becoming more enthusiastic, as a result of involvement in initial teacher education and training, teachers may take on new ideas for teaching.

This is certainly not a new phenomenon, but is one with probably more potential nowadays. Students bring with them aspects of subject expertise along with a range of teaching strategies, and in some cases teachers report that they themselves have learned fresh ways to construct learning opportunities or develop teaching strategies. There is often an expectation that staff will be refreshed by mentoring – the Heineken effect. Shaw (1993) suggests that mentoring can be seen as a process which contributes to the professional development of all participants, including pupils. A question raised in the Mentoring in Schools project by one of its participants deserves attention, namely, whether it is reasonable to expect that the mentor and the student should both gain professionally from the experience.

Arguably teachers' professional development is simply a spin-off from school-based training. It frequently occurs, yet remains no more than a happy coincidence. Alternatively, it could be argued that the phenomenon is so widely recognised, and so consistently cited as a desired outcome for schools, that it should be built into the structure of school-based training, and clear opportunities provided for teachers to discuss their own professional development. Recognition of their work via accreditation is sometimes cited as another benefit. One result has been the growth of formal structures. Such recognition is all very well, but it begs the question of what teachers do with their certificates and accreditation when they receive them. It may be a fair reward for their early contributions, but then what?

Evaluating and appraising practice

Hosting a student in the classroom, as evidenced in the Mentoring in Schools project, provokes questions such as. 'Am I doing this the right way?' and 'Why am I doing this?' Teachers regularly experience an increase in their ability to evaluate their own and students' practice through discussion and written feed-back. The area of written feedback is one which many mentors find difficult at the beginning of their mentoring career, because of lack of confidence and in some cases a reluctance to make public their thoughts and advice. Campbell *et al.* (1998 in press) found that 'one of the main differences in the roles of tutors and teachers, namely that of promoting in students, systematic, critical evaluation of practice in order to refine, renew and develop teaching' needs further investigation Campbell and Kane (1996a) supported the idea that primary school culture requires students to 'fit in' rather than critically question and evaluate. If this were so, and remains so, it is important that collaborative and joint approaches between schools and higher education develop in order to promote criticality and to avoid a 'division of labour' approach to teacher training.

Networking

Clearly teachers value the opportunity to meet teachers from other schools and LEAs. Most partnerships provide a forum for purposeful dialogues about teacher education, children's learning and the management and organisation of student placements. Networking is increasing and sometimes compensating for the loss of the old LEA networks. This aspect is probably particularly motivating for teachers looking for professional discourse and opportunities to exchange ideas.

The Partnership factor

Partnership has messages for school-based continuing professional development. In recent years there has been an increase in school-based professional development activity and expectations of teachers have changed, requiring professional development activity to be an integral part of the job. Partly this is due to the many imposed innovations in schools which require immediate responses, and partly it is due to the development of professional awareness as a result of changes in the initial education of teachers which encourage thinking about, and evaluation of, practice.

The spectre of an OFSTED inspection normally heralds much 'instant' or 'quick-fix' school-based professional development, putting hard-pressed teachers under even more pressure and exacerbating innovation overload. The move to school-based professional development, rather than higher-education-based provision or the now-dwindling LEA course programme or the long-lost HMI courses, is also affected by partnership initiatives which focus on teachers' roles in mentoring and in supporting students in schools. It is also a result of central policies which, having promoted 'on the job' training for student teachers, are now seemingly promoting 'on the job' development for experienced teachers. This move to apprenticeship models and 'do it yourself' CPD encourages a view of teaching which appears to value the more technical aspects of teaching and appears not to encourage the systematic and critical evaluation approach characteristic of higher education. Arguably, it must be seen as a threat to the professionalism of teachers. That learning from each other and engaging in concrete, precise talk about teaching are valuable is not in dispute, but it is not sufficient to constitute professional development; nor is reflection on practice by itself enough, as discussed by Day (1993).

The challenge for schools and higher education is to harness both theory and practice in the context of school-based professional development and university-based provision. The idea of a 'course' as the usual experience is frequently now no longer what schools want. What may well be required from partnership is consultancy on whole-school issues or departmental concerns which need not necessarily come from the particular partnership university itself but might be brokered by that university pulling in other schools known to have the skills required for the specific consultancy. Exchange and peer review with other schools are further possibilities which offer insight into how partnership might contribute to school-based professional development.

Mentor as researcher

Another aspect of teacher development through mentoring is Edwards and Collison's (1996) idea of the mentor as researcher, gathering data and reflecting on the mentoring process, through case study and action research. In similar ways mentoring has led many teachers recently into Master's level studies or enquiries as they follow lines of investigation suggested to them by their experience in school-based training. Wilma is the classic example. Derek's loyalty too was linked to the university through postgraduate study.

It is not always appropriate to focus teacher research exclusively on the process of 'doing' mentoring. It might be more relevant to development of children's literacy or numeracy to look at how students might be assisted in their school-based work in say literacy or numeracy, i.e. the effect of being 'done to'. Collaborative enquiry with students is also another possibility which is entirely appropriate, given that many courses now require students to undertake an action research enquiry as part of their course work. The tale in Chapter 6, 'Triumph and disaster', shows both the problems and the potential of students as researchers. Put a better student with Mark and the PCS could have really taken off. Edwards and Collison (1996) support mentors' co-enquiry with students in investigating dilemmas and puzzles and developing appropriate strategies for solutions. These enquires would represent a set of opportunities to explore and make explicit teachers' professional knowledge, or craft knowledge, as discussed in the commentary upon Mike's story.

Tensions and dilemmas in mentoring

The four mentors at Jemima Johnston were clearly feeling under pressure and for a variety of reasons. Throughout discussions about school-based training in schools, colleges and universities, 'having the time' features prominently as an issue causing tension and stress. Mentoring clearly requires structured time for proper discussions. When fitted into and around a busy day with no formal release it can only increase the workload of already busy teachers. If a mentor is non-class-based, time is more easily available, but in the straitened financial circumstances of recent years this has become less and less likely and has tended to take senior teachers' time away from other responsibilities to staff and children, which it will be recalled was part of Wilma's distress. Tomlinson (1995) acknowledges the stress experienced by mentors, not only because of pressure of work and time factors, but also because of the interactive nature of the interpersonal aspects of mentoring.

Status is also a concern which can cause tension. The position of the mentor is often that of a senior member of staff. In one situation in the Mentoring in Schools project, where the mentor was not in the senior management team, he experienced difficulties in managing difficult situations (Campbell and Kane (1996a)). Two of the Jemima Johnston mentors have a clear status: Wilma as Deputy Head and Meg as Head of the KS1 section. Mark's position in the 'real' hierarchy was ambivalent. Ironically, perhaps the most confident of all was Tom, whose status was largely self-defined and who operated quasi-autonomously – at least until things went wrong. Wilma was clearly torn about her other duties while being vulnerable to assault in her mentoring role by Class Next Door. Without her status as Deputy Head, her multiple involvement in the school could well have torn her apart. Meg was much clearer about her status. It certainly included the freedom to say 'no' to having a student, or to demand a rest.

There has been a gradual realisation that the proper in-school management of school-based training is a necessary condition for success. The placement of students in appropriate classrooms, the organisation of supply cover, handling relationships and communications with university staff, record-keeping and reporting, and communication with governors and parents about school-based training are only a few of the tasks which need attention. Experience suggests that having someone like Wilma, with an overview and responsibility for monitoring and coordinating the mentoring of students, is a very valuable resource. It should be built into the management structure of a school engaged in school-based training, as a designated responsibility, possibly even at head teacher level.

The need for clear roles, especially the role of the class teacher–mentor, is conventionally recognised as being important, but one area where controversy has been acknowledged is whether mentors should be paid individually or whether the money should go to the school to be spent as and when. Varying solutions have been found nationally. A climate of cooperation may be seen as a necessary condition for good mentoring, together with the full support of staff. 'Whole-school mentoring' and 'the mentoring school' have emerged as worthwhile aims. Both concepts could be seen as idealistic, but nonetheless each is surely worth striving for. The logic of this would seem to be to view the income accruing to a school as being a 'whole-school' resource.

The 'mentoring school' becomes more than just a worthwhile objective and becomes desirable both structurally and functionally as the system begins to grapple with the problem of mentor 'turnover': the replacement of mentors who are either promoted (a regular occurrence) or who 'burn-out' or who move schools. Funding for mentor training and preparation no longer takes this movement into account, with 1997–98 funding being earmarked for adapting to changes required by Circular 10/97. Yet mentor development, renewal and extension are very real needs which do not seem to figure in current partnership financial costings. Welton, Howson and Bines (1995: 222) summarise how many schools and universities feel: 'For the concept of partnership to be more than empty rhetoric those responsible for the strategic planning of teacher development must ensure sufficient funds to enable successful training to take place.'

Because of the pressures on funding and the failure to set in place a rational, national approach, many successful partnerships, up and down the country, continue to survive largely on good will. There has to be a question of how long such a situation can go on, in the face of more imposed changes and increasing inspections and re-inspections. It is an issue raised by Sir Stewart Sutherland in Report No. 10 to the Dearing Enquiry (1997) which calls for the funding situation to be addressed.

FURTHER READING

Tomlinson, P. (1995) *Understanding Mentoring: Reflective Strategies for School-Based Training*, Milton Keynes: Open University Press, provides a comprehensive and useful text about mentoring. Despite the fact that it is secondary focused, it still has much to offer to primary orientated readers. Chapter 4 'The effective facilitator: interpersonal aspects of mentoring' relates well to this story of mentors under pressure.

The management of partnership and school-based training is discussed in Bines, H. and Welton, J. (eds) (1995) *Managing Partnership in Teacher Training and Development*, London: Routledge. Chapters 4 and 5 are particularly related to issues concerning primary schools.

Glover, D. and Mardle, G. (1996) 'Issues in the management of mentoring', in McIntyre, D. and Hagger, H. *Mentors in Schools: Developing the Profession of Teaching*, London: David Fulton Publishers, cover most of the issues raised above.

In Rhodes, G. (1994) 'Managing the beginning teacher in school', in Wilkin, M. and Sankey, D. (eds) (1994) *Collaboration and Transition in Initial Teacher Training*, London: Kogan Page, there is a useful discussion about managing students.

For an interesting chapter on mentors as researchers see Chapter 9 in Edwards, A. and Collison, J. (1996) *Mentoring and Developing Practice in Primary Schools: Supporting Student Teacher Learning in School*. Milton Keynes: Open University Press.

For a discussion of mentoring and staff development see Kelly, M., Beck, T., Ap Thomas, J. (1992) 'Mentoring as a staff development activity', in Wilkin, M. (ed.) *Mentoring in Schools*, London: Kogan Page.

CHAPTER 8

Partners: stormy weather

For a change Derek had come to visit me at our campus. I had thought he deserved a little trip out. We were to discuss the forthcoming Staff Development Day at the school and then I was going to take him over the road for lunch. 'Over the road' was quite a prepossessing restaurant with an engaging ambience. The alternative was to visit the refectory on campus. 'Over the road' was actually cheaper and part of its positive ambience was that when you sat down with visitors, a member of the kitchen staff didn't march up to you and announce with clarion-call firmness, 'It's fish'.

In any case, I wanted to find some way to express my appreciation to Derek, who had from the outset been one of our more supportive Heads, although occasionally his robust humour did take some patience to live with. His favourite theme was the out-of-date, out-of-touch, ivory-towered uselessness of some university tutors, present company excepted, of course. Quite apart from present company, he made a surprising amount of use of other tutors, whom he latched on to when they visited the school. He'd gobbled Trish alive and at one time I'd begun to think she was on *their* staff, not ours. But, as he explained, she wasn't your normal run of university tutor. She'd been an Advisory Teacher with his LEA and as everyone knew you didn't get to be an Advisory Teacher unless your feet were firmly planted on the ground. Derek had been an Advisory Teacher shortly before he became an Acting Head. The trouble with university tutors, he'd told me, was that their feet were firmly planted in the sky. And he'd laughed uproariously. I myself had smiled politely.

It was not always easy to see where Derek's dislike of university tutors came from, since he seemed to exempt most people every time he stumbled across a name. I had decided that the explanation was nurture not nature. What he really had it in for was educational theory. He himself had been trained at a time when the four disciplines were big in education and no course was complete or respectable without substantial dollops of psychology, sociology, philosophy and history with 'education' stuck in front of them or 'of education' after them. Frequently in his era, the course components had been delivered to the assembled hordes with CCTV facilities coping with a significant overspill population, since even our barn of a hall couldn't cope with the total cohort. Not for the first session or two anyway. After a relatively short time the size of the hall had mysteriously seemed to expand to cope with the numbers of students arriving. This was whole-class teaching at its finest. All it took was one tutor, and a colleague at the beginning to pass around the handouts. It was also team-teaching at its most sophisticated, although a microphone would have helped. As the OHP gained a firmer and firmer grip on educational pedagogy, presentation was increasingly honed so that the handout tutor acquired the additional responsibilities of switching the OHP on. It stayed on for the full hour. Thus a generation of students who could not hear was replaced by an increasingly sophisticated generation who could neither hear nor see. Except of course for the first few rows. As is long-established practice, the OHTs were dutifully read out in a stumbling monotone, thus making the first few rows who could already both hear and see doubly advantaged – or disadvantaged. Opinion varied. Naturally enough by the end of the year only the first few rows were needed, although there was usually a good attendance for the mass lecture on group work. In the final year the four disciplines gave way to Educational Issues when the staff–student ratio, boosted by the economics of scale which the mass lectures of previous years made possible, now gave way to smaller class sizes. The students would now be in small groups for their lectures.

All this had scarred Derek for life. In vain did I regularly explain to him that contemporary practice, and the contribution of educational theory, bore no resemblance whatsoever to the travesty of the days of the disciplines. Incidentally, I have often wondered what it was about practice in the 70s (the 60s, in my view, are wrongly stigmatised) which earned the label of 'trendy' let alone 'lefty'. Most trendy lefties I have known, which is not many because my experience has been that lefties are rarely trendy, wouldn't have been seen dead in a mass lecture, and had little or no time for the educational disciplines. However, Derek was locked firmly into his early to mid 70s past and was not for turning. In vain did I point out that it was only a few years since he had completed his MEd with us, on a course which was highly interactive and practitioner based but nonetheless owed not a little to educational theory. His mind was made up: school-based good: education tutors bad. He did not count me as an education tutor because, as he said, I had a proper subject to talk about. His *bête noir* was Jeremy, whom he associated with what he consistently described as 'that rubbish – Extended Professional Studies'. He had a view of EPS as 'a tarted-up version of all that junk we used to do when I was at college, but with new jargon', which he reckoned we inflicted on the students 'to make common-sense trivia seem important or to make sensible practice unintelligible and inaccessible to new teachers'. He had from an early stage tagged EPS as a 'job creation scheme', which he said was no bad thing if it kept 'self-important, pompous idiots like Jeremy off our backs' in the schools.

That said, for him mentoring was a good thing and the extra time spent in schools was time truly well spent. He had been supportive from the beginning and had continued to be so. He had received tutors graciously, except for

Jeremy, from whom he had once physically run away shouting, 'Sorry, can't stop, there's a problem with the boiler'. Most of our tutors he got on really well with and it was clear he held them in some respect. I have to confess, too, that he was right about Jeremy who had a tendency – more than a tendency, actually a well-honed practice – to buttonhole people and pontificate, while consistently refusing to answer a direct question. A colleague had once described him as 'a man without an exit line'. I supposed that was why people ran away from him. I had done it myself.

'Nice to visit the ivory towers,' said Derek as he walked into my room. 'I hope I'm not too early. Do you want a minute or two to sort out the mail, if you've just arrived?' It was 11 a.m. and I decided to ignore him. Instead I made him a cup of coffee.

'Sorry it's not in a china cup,' I said. 'No LMS bonanza for us, you know – oh, and I'm sorry I've no bourbon biscuits.' China cups and bourbon biscuits were the speciality of the house in Derek's office. 'Sometimes I'm very embarrassed when you and other heads visit me in this hovel. More and more I wish I was back working in a school.'

The sparring went on for a while. We got on well and I liked him. I think he liked me but under the banter we were coming from different standpoints.

The purpose of his visit, I have explained, was to prepare for the Staff Development Day at which I was to be the guest speaker. It was a sign of Derek's commitment that he, like several other heads, had allocated one of the teacher days to an examination of school-based training and the concept of 'a whole-school approach'. I was to open up the day, talking for about an hour, reviewing where we had got to and picking out what I saw as the key issues for attention.

'What I want,' said Derek, 'is to make the entire operation much more systematic. I've been thinking it all through and I've a number of ideas. Some of them are lowish level day-to-day things but there's one thing that's a bit more avante garde.' I remembered that Wilma had said at the mentors' meeting that she thought Derek was up to something. Time would tell. I gestured to him to elaborate.

'First off, we need a policy on school-based training and mentoring. We don't actually have a policy. If anything, we're operating to your policy. All we've got is a decision. We decided to go along working with you to bring about the implementation of Circular 14/93. That's a fair enough statement isn't it?'

'Broadly.'

'Now we know Circular 14/93 is for the scrapheap. All that stuff about competences will be jettisoned. Yes?'

'Maybe.'

'There's going to be a national curriculum which all teacher-training places are going to have to follow. Am I right?'

'Broadly.'

'And then at the end of the course the students are going to have to achieve standards. Have I understood it?'

'Maybe.'

'What do you take "standards" to be?'

'Words,' I said, 'new words to take the place of competences.'

'You're unduly cynical,' offered Derek.

'Battle-scarred by constant change,' I replied, but I was quite surprised at the level of knowledge and understanding he had about something which so far only existed in draft and the fate of which hung on a new government. I decided to let him expose his thinking. So far, I wasn't sure exactly where he was going. I had begun to smell OFSTED in all this. Whenever head teachers begin to talk about policies, the word OFSTED flashes in multicoloured lights. Several of them I know had regularly exchanged policies and most had a filing cabinet or box file labelled 'OFSTED: Policies'. Now I guessed I knew what it was that Wilma had thought Derek was up to. With OFSTED still to come, he wanted a policy on initial teacher-training in the context of the school's involvement in partnership with us. And he wanted me to help him write it and sell it to the staff. 'Well, fair enough,' was my silent reaction. He was only doing what we wanted all schools to do. He launched into his exposition.

'We need a clear policy,' he said. 'There are a number of issues which a school needs to consider before entering into any new arrangements for school-based ITT.'

'Yes,' I said. 'If you remember we went over a lot of them four years ago at the meeting when I spoke.'

He gave me a funny look which I didn't quite understand.

'That was your agenda. That was all very new to us.'

It was my turn to give *him* a funny look.

He continued. 'There are issues to do with staff involvement: the choice of mentors and the mentors' role, the role of the classteacher or other teachers, how ITE will be managed within schools, how the school's involvement will contribute to the professional development of its staff. You have to remember that at present the support of ITT students is not a contractual duty under the current School Teachers' Pay and Conditions Document'.

How could I forget? It was my recurring nightmare that the government would try to make it so and partnership would fall about us in ruins.

Derek went on, 'There are other things that a school has to think about: student accommodation for one – ours is a very small staffroom; library facilities – we don't have any books on pedagogy – they're all back here in your library; use of other materials – students eat reprographic stuff. Then there are day-to-day practicalities, of which disruption is the greatest. Taking students adds to the workload of the Head and Deputy Head and one has to evaluate the wisdom of taking on this extra responsibility which goes along with the role of teacher educator. Moreover, we need to ask ourselves how many students we should have in the school over a year, and set in place arrangements for monitoring to ensure that specific pupils are not involved too often.'

'Where had he got that one from?' I wondered. This was quite sophisticated stuff. He went on.

'This particular policy when I, we, have worked it out will have to go to the Governors. They will need to be satisfied that consultation with the staff has taken place. They will need to consider whether responsibilities are clear and how the school would handle a student who was causing problems. If the Governing Body sought to enter into any contract they'd need to be clear whether such a contract need comply with the financial regulations of the LEA, and would normally be part of the LMS scheme. Should the Chair of Governors sign any contract?'

He *had* been thinking! I was impressed. I could see that my potential contribution to the Staff Development Day was going to have to focus on major issues which were essentially open-ended – things neither of us had really worked out any answers to yet. Derek wasn't finished. He was also concerned about parents. He wanted parents in his policy. The OFSTED lights were flashing again. He was well aware that parents were already concerned that effective and experienced teachers were being diverted from teaching pupils to acting as mentors for students. He had picked up rumbles about children being taught extensively by students. Some pupils and parents, it seemed, perceived this as damaging to the pupils' opportunities. Inevitably, it seemed it was the more ambitious and articulate parents who had pursued this. Some had gone so far as to suggest that the school seemed to be serving the students rather than meeting its principal responsibility to its pupils. Others had intuitively grasped the photocopying and reprographic issue and were concerned that resources were being used for ITE rather than other areas. All this Derek spelt out to me succinctly.

Finally, he came to what for me, because of my particular role, was the crunch: the choice of mentors. The model we had evolved over the years was that of a 'class teacher as mentor' model but we had also established the need to have someone – in their case, it was Wilma – who discharged an overarching role and who 'managed' the partnership arrangements, which included the use of the funding we were transferring and the organising of supply teachers. In our earliest thinking we had had a view of the Wilma role as more detached and external, away from the day-to-day routines of the classroom. It did not take us long to decide that, when push came to shove, there could be no ignoring the class teacher. The class teacher was at the heart of everything. Accordingly the class teacher should be the mentor. None of this meant that there was not a need for someone to manage the arrangements. It was just that the role of super-mentor – or more accurately 'supra-mentor' – common in secondary schools, appeared to most of those involved to be anomalous in a primary school. In the event there had been a budget crisis at Jemima Johnston and Wilma had had to become a class teacher again so all the bits of the jigsaw fell into place. That had still left open the question of precisely which class teachers would be mentors. Not everyone was suitable – or so it seemed to be generally agreed. Time and events had thrown up Meg from the KS1 section together with Tom, Mark and Wilma, who were KS2-based, though Mark had good experience at KS1. Then there was Damien 'waiting in the wings.'

As Derek said, 'We've struck lucky with our mentors but it didn't have to work out so well.'

I closed my eyes and thought of Tom.

'No, Derek, it didn't. We were lucky.'

'The way I've been thinking,' said Derek, 'in my policy . . . '

'Oh ho,' I thought, 'what's this "my" policy? So much for a whole-school approach after widespread discussion among staff, governors and parents.'

' . . . I think somewhere it should be spelt out what we see . . . '

Back to 'we' again, I was relieved to notice.

' . . . are the qualities possessed by mentors or needed by mentors.'

I was thinking that somewhere in this conversation I was going to have to give him a more detailed report of the meeting which I'd had the previous week with his four key mentors. I'd briefly gone through the content of the meeting with him after it was over but mainly to the effect that we ought to be looking for a couple of new mentors. That was good policy anyway and it was clear from the way Derek was talking and the direction in which he seemed to be going that that was how he saw it too. He saw it, bless him, as widening the pool of experience. Soon I was going to have to break it to him that Wilma was hoping to get a Headship out of the interviews which were scheduled that day and the day after, that Mark saw mentoring as a lift up the ladder and that he too hoped to be off, while Meg wanted a rest. Only Tom could be relied upon faithfully to soldier on.

'We need more mentors, but I think we need to be clearer about the qualities required.' He was repeating himself. 'Between you and me,' he said, 'I'm not sure Tom's really right for it and I'd be quite happy to sideline him.'

'You wish.'

'Why do you say that?'

'I'll tell you later. I'm sorry I interrupted your flow. Go on, spell out the qualities of a good classroom teacher–mentor – as you see them.'

'Well, you're the expert and no doubt you've worked it all out from what you've seen, and to be honest it's that sort of thing that I hope you'll be talking about at the Staff Development Day.'

I wasn't sure that I fancied that but I recognised it as something which we did have to get our heads around, and then confront, if that wasn't too strong a word.

'But my first thoughts, for what they are worth, are these. In general terms, I recognise that there are a number of highly particular skills students need, or competences. Is that the word? Have I got the jargon right?' He was his old self again.

'Standards,' I said wisely. 'We expect everyone to work to Standards nowadays, this year anyway, and probably next, so we might as well start applying the new vocabulary to all appropriate situations.'

'OK,' he said. 'Serve one to you. I'll let it pass but here's my shortlist.' He fished out a piece of paper to which he referred as he spoke. 'Mentors must be willing to consider and try new ideas. They must be constructively critical of what's going on in their classrooms. They must be willing to evaluate their teaching methods and see that doing so is part of their career-long development. Above all they must recognise how this development will be encouraged and assisted by being involved in a process of initial training which stresses from the beginning the importance of reflecting on practice. In short they must themselves be well developed reflective practitioners.'

I looked at him. Dumbstruck. Was this Saul on the way to Damascus? Whence this blinding conversion? Not only had he used the words 'reflective practitioner', but he had used them without a curl of the lip. He had used them with respect, reverentially even. He had cited them as a desirable aim. I knew what I wanted to say.

'Well, colour me happy, Derek, you old cynical hypocrite, you two-faced opportunist. I intend to recommend you for the vicarship of Bray. You theoretical mountebank, you. You've finally seen what it is that we've been banging on about.'

Because we have known each other for many years and because, for all his rustic approaches, he had been a good MEd student, I did say exactly that, but he only smiled.

'I thought you might like that,' he said, 'but I'm not at all interested in being a vicar.'

'I'm glad. It wouldn't suit you.'

'No, what I'm interested in is being the lead school in a SCITT scheme.'

There was a profound and gobsmacked silence. I gave him the hardest of hard stares. School-Centred Initial Teacher Training – SCITT – the Patten-reared brainchild of the Tory Government and the foster child of the TTA. SCITT – the acronym was anathema to me as someone totally dedicated to Partnership, someone who really believed in Partnership, someone who felt it was working, could work better but still offered the best hope for the future in bringing about improvements in the quality of teacher training. Alas, those of us who had believed in it had had to develop it against a background of apathy from the very government which had launched it. They didn't want Partnership, nor it seemed did the TTA – except under sufferance as a temporary measure. No, it was to SCITT that the term 'pioneering' was consistently attached. SCITT – announced in March 1994, regulated for in May, launched in September, evaluated in October and expanded in December. SCITT – the DIY model wherein schools took the funding to themselves and purchased the services of HE only as and when and if they fancied. SCITT – which could not guarantee students on PGCE-style training an award, only Qualified Teacher Status. SCITT – which would really show the dilettantes of higher education how it was done. SCITT – the favourite child – weak, undeveloped, undernourished but which took good, valuable schools away from Partnership at a time when HE institutions were scouring their catchment areas for potential partnerships. SCITT – supported and subsidised by the TTA, but nonetheless a disaster zone in some places as far as primary education was concerned. Could I be hearing this right?

'He's up to something,' Wilma had said.

Derek was by now beginning to look more than a little embarrassed. I spread my arms and shook my head in puzzled bewilderment. I could hardly get anything out. The words wouldn't come.

'SCITT!' I said. Then a big pause. 'Why?'

And then the whole sorry story came out.

'I don't want you to think we're deserting you; we'll be using your services, naturally; we wouldn't want to work with anyone else.'

'You've got a surprise coming, brother,' I said, like a tough cool character in TV films, except I didn't actually say it, I just thought it. What I said was, 'Tell me more.'

'I got the idea from talking to the Head at St Michael's.' St Michael's is a church school, C of E, in the south of the city. The parents are not short of a bob or two and although it has its usual run of problems – sometimes there seem to be as many broken homes in the affluent suburbs as there are in the inner city – by and large it provides a good teaching environment and like Jemima Johnston has joined willingly in the partnership arrangements and has provided a good level of support. I was intrigued about whether the SCITT heresy was sweeping the city.

'Colin Crombie, the head there, said that when OFSTED came they were very interested in the school's involvement with initial teacher training. He seemed to think that it had counted towards their good report. Anyway, last month Colin was invited to some big do or other down south, first class travel, all expenses paid, lavish hospitality, the works. Chris Woodhead was running the show along with the woman who runs the TTA, Anthea Miller . . . '

'Millett.'

'Whatever. Blunkett's Number 2 was there – Byers – and it seems it was a gathering of all the primary schools which had had the best OFSTED reports and the idea was to encourage them to be SCITT schools. Woodhead said he'd get some money from the Prince's Trust to top up the money they got from the TTA. Colin said that the not-too-subtle message was that you lot in higher education have messed up teacher training and it was up to the schools with the best OFSTED reports to put it right. And there were some videos available on how to do it properly, well, teaching reading anyway.'

I recognised this for a somewhat garbled account. I'd had other accounts, one from Colin actually, who had been vastly irritated by the event, and I knew I could set Derek right on a couple of points, but why should I have to? When we were desperately seeking to establish Partnership and recruit schools, why were important and influential people, perhaps accidentally, perhaps with the best of motives, undermining our work? At least 97 per cent of new teachers were coming through the partnership system. 'Didn't these major figures in education want it to work for goodness sake?' I raged inwardly. For three or four years we had been struggling to establish Partnership and school-based training. It was an expensive model which had received no financial support. What had been achieved in those years had been achieved in large part through a massive contribution of goodwill from schools for blatantly inadequate reward. Who was inviting representatives from those schools to expensive jollies? Why was it only the SCITT schools which received a TTA subsidy? Why had it all been done in secret anyway, without a word to the rest of the system? 150 schools had been invited; many had not been involved in partnership. Why not? Where were they when we needed them? The remainder had. What could possibly be achieved by coaxing them away from Partnership, through flattery and financial inducements? All these thoughts ran through my head as I turned to Derek. He clearly thought he had found a way to get a good result from OFSTED. He'd be better off with Oxfam.

'They weren't the schools with the best 150 reports,' I said, 'it was the best SATs.'

Derek digested this and a penny dropped softly in the distance.

'But that's not fair,' said Derek. 'We do OK in the SATs but with our catchment area, we can't possibly do as well as St Michael's. And,' he added, 'I'm not sure that the best training for students is an exclusive diet of schools whose social composition guarantees good SATs results.'

I made no comment, but I couldn't resist twisting the knife.

'You'll get double OFSTED as a SCITT school, you know.'

'Double? Why?'

'You'll get the standard visit to inspect the school and they may or may not talk to you about your teacher-training policy, but you'll also get inspected by the OFSTED Teacher Education and Training Team. Every provider – and

SCITT schools become classed as providers automatically – is inspected under the same criteria – you SCITTers the same as us. The difference is that the schools, especially the lead schools, have to carry the burden of the inspection.'

I reached across, fished out and passed him a document of mind-blowing complexity which those of us in teacher-training had grown to love.

'Try this,' I said, flicking it open to the key page. 'This is the Framework for the Assessment of Quality and Standards. You see those 17 cells – you get inspected on every single one of those,' I lied, 'and graded, and the results are published nationally. Before, those inspectors aren't soft touches like your OFSTED lot. These are "bona fide" HMI. They are very courteous, very polite, but they operate in search mode at a level somewhere between the SS and the Gestapo. They'd have found Anne Frank, no problem.'

'You're talking your usual exaggerated rubbish,' he said, but without conviction. 'I bet what you've said is a caricature of the truth – at best.'

'Really? Derek, let me just read to you a few extracts from the very latest report to be published.' This time I reached across to a pile of yellow perils – OFSTED 'Primary Sweep' reports.

'How about these for encouragement?' and I proceeded to read a few choice excerpts which I had marked. These included the following:

> 'In a quarter of the lessons observed, teaching was unsatisfactory.'
> 'The taught course in teaching studies and in English is not sufficiently linked to school-based training.'
> 'Training in English . . . is unsatisfactory.'
> 'Some students do not have experience of teaching beginning reading.'

I raised my head, 'This is in a school-centred course, Derek.'

> 'The consortium does not have a common approach to training.' (OFSTED 1997)

I let him digest these comments, especially the latter.

'That'll be your fault if it happens in your consortium, Derek.'

There was a silence. Then Derek spoke.

'We're better than that,' he said, and it was certainly true what he said, 'and we'd be working with you.'

I shook my head.

'You'd desert us?' he said indignantly, 'after all the work we've done together and after the way we immediately joined in Partnership and supported you. That's shameful.'

'No, it's not Derek. We just don't have the resources. We're stretched to the absolute limit and all our commitment is to Partnership. Every tutor we have is needed to go flat out just to make Partnership work, and we are making it work. Colin isn't off SCITTing is he?'

'Well, no, but I was hoping he'd join in.'

'He's twelve miles away,' I said, 'and twelve million miles away from you ideologically, it would seem. He told me he thought the junket was a disgrace. Full of snide cracks about higher education and he awarded it at least two bargepole status.'

Derek look puzzled. I explained.

'You are familiar with the saying "I wouldn't touch it with a bargepole"?'

Derek nodded.

'Colin wouldn't touch this scheme with two bargepoles – at least. Quite apart from the unacceptable sales pitch, he told me he reckoned it was too much work, too much disruption, too much potential aggro, especially parent aggro, and it would be worst of all for the lead school. In any case he didn't want to be led by another school. He wanted to be led, if that's the right word, by his neighbouring university.'

'I'm made of sterner stuff than that,' said Derek. 'I can handle all that. I reckon we're a good school, we're good at teacher training – with your help admittedly – and we ought to play our part in training the next generation.'

'You *are* playing your part,' I urged, 'a vital, crucial part, with us. Quite frankly we need you. I read you that one report. There are plenty more and there was an overall OFSTED report you know, in August 1995, on SCITTs, mainly secondary (OFSTED 1995a). It was pretty unenthusiastic. It's no surprise it was published in August – in the same week as the A levels, incidentally. That September, a month later, OFSTED published a more positive report on Partnership (OFSTED 1995b). After that came all the secondary schemes' reports and then the Primary Sweep and partnership came out looking pretty good, really. Why wreck it?'

'I'm not wrecking it,' said Derek, 'I'm building on the good work we've done and I'm taking it forward.'

There was clearly no shifting him. I could see that this was the real agenda for the Staff Development Day. Wilma had been right. Derek was up to something. I tried a final shot.

'What do the staff think?' I said. 'Are your tried and trusted mentors with you on this?'

Derek shifted uneasily. 'We haven't discussed it yet. That's partly what the Staff Development Day is all about. We'll thrash it out next Monday.'

I was fresh from my meeting with the gang of four. I knew things he didn't know. 'What if they don't like the idea?'

'Then we'll stick with what we've got, but I'll think it will be a missed opportunity.'

Part of me smiled. I rated his chances at something the sunny side of zero. What troubled me – and troubled me deeply – was that Derek's plan could just be the last straw to break the back of hitherto willing, but increasingly burdened, camels. Yet again I cursed SCITT and its unhelpful, shortsighted protagonists. This was the last thing we needed. It could unsettle the Partnership more generally. Other schools would hear about Derek's plan and maybe share his view that here was an OFSTED ace in the hole. The Staff Development Day had suddenly assumed major significance.

'OK, Derek. You'll do your thing next Monday, I'll do mine. We don't want to be seen arguing in public. We've got work to do. Monday's going to take a lot of planning, so let's get down to it.'

He nodded agreement and reached into his briefcase for his draft documents. Cunning is Derek, underneath it all. I reached for a blank piece of paper.

'Here's what we'll do,' I said, and quickly sketched out a big circle, a blob in the middle and lines radiating out to the perimeter.

'What on earth is that?'

'It's a wheel,' I said. 'We're going to reinvent it.'

COMMENTARY AND MATTERS FOR DISCUSSION

Whole-school approaches to mentoring

Throughout the tales and their commentaries we have touched on the concept of whole-school mentoring and the notion of 'the mentoring school'. What does it mean? What does it take to bring it about? This was the narrator's agenda for the Staff Development Day.

There has been a gradual realisation and recognition of the importance to mentoring of school ethos to mentoring; and the attitudes of staff, parents and governors, the impact of the culture of the school, the norms of behaviour, accepted work practices, expectations of the inhabitants and visitors to the environment, and the language used in schools, all contribute to and shape the mentoring experiences of teachers and students.

While the concept of a primary school specific culture is germane, a different concept of 'the mentoring school' is valuable, and is one which Watkins and Whalley (1995) argue supports the most effective mentoring. It would generally be agreed that the style of the school is important. Where it is consultative and inclusive, mentoring prospers. In a 'mentoring school' one would look for positive attitudes to working as a team, a warm environment where openness and trust and honesty were apparent, where staff and pupils lived by the rules. Arguably, there needs to be an openness to criticism, a willingness to accept critical comments, and in the end teachers should be able to work together. The most negative feature would be complacency: a smug, self-satisfied contentment with what already exists. There has to be a recognition of the need to change and develop and to grow. Happily, complacent schools rarely are prepared to make a commitment to involve themselves in partnership. When they do, they want it to be on their terms. The partner HE-provider and the students are both expected to adapt and to fit in. In such circumstances, Partnership rarely works.

In the 'fresh look at training relationships' and the role of schools in teacher education, Edwards and Collison (1996) calls upon the five learning disciplines of Senge (1992) which emphasise process and continuous development and counsel against quick-fix solutions. Changes in educational policy in the last twenty years are relevant. The current climate is a long way from the past notions of an individualistic and private profession of teaching. While most primary schools seem much more collaborative in nature, some caution should be exercised as many complex interpersonal relationships and networks exist in primary schools which can cause difficulties for newcomers. Schools are at different stages of development, and collaboration is often not easy.

There are messages from abroad, e.g. Fullan (1991), who characterises high quality collaboration as 'continuous learners in a community of interactive professionals'. However, notions of the 'mentoring school' need much further investigation and possible reconceptualisation, particularly with regard to the possible conflicting interests of teachers, students and pupils. Fullan (1993) in his analysis of the change process, as related to schools participating in partnerships with universities and school districts in Canada, states that schools should be assessed against criteria which consist of learning conditions for all educators. Stoll and Fink (1996) report positively on a Canadian Learning Consortium, first established in 1988 as a collaborative teacher education partnership between four school districts and two HE institutions, which 'opened up a continuum of interlinked professional development from pre-service through to leadership'.

It is to this area that we must look for future direction and future development, in the face of a radical review of CPD and the evolution of Partnership.

School-Centred Initial Teacher Training (SCITT)

Derek had a different agenda from the narrator. It is unlikely that many staff would share it. It is a fair assertion that the vast majority of schools do not want to go it alone, confirmed by others, e.g. Downes (1996), Bines and Welton (1995). This was the message of the Mentoring in Schools project, Campbell and Kane (1996b). Most schools seem actively to want a strong higher education presence in the school-based training of teachers, and value the distinctive contribution which higher education tutors make to initial teacher education. They doubt that they can provide all that is required for the education of student teachers. Where effective collaboration exists between schools and higher education, there is a high quality of student experience, which is characterised by a recognition of the complexities of educating teachers. This results in a supportive, yet challenging, model of supervision of students.

There is also a clearer understanding by both parties of the various roles involved in effective school-based teacher training. The high quality class teacher is a resource too precious to misuse. Enhancing the quality of supervision and partnership is costly in energy, time and money and it is recognised that time spent mentoring is time away from teaching pupils, which has implications for staffing and teachers' workloads. There is also a need in schools to manage and co-ordinate school-based teacher training, so as to be efficient in the use of the transferred funding, in the selection of staff, in monitoring and evaluating staff development, in the provision of subject specific support for students, in the tracking of student impact on specific classes and, not least, in making supply cover arrangements. Derek was right about those issues.

Schools have become increasingly aware of the extra work involved in partnership. Will many schools opt for SCITT? SCITT schemes have been around since 1993. What do we know about them? We know that SCITT has been heavily promoted by the TTA and HMCI. Both have put pen to paper to try to recruit 'excellent primary schools' as illustrated in the dialogue with Derek and as evidenced in recent letters to selected primary schools, Woodhead (1997) and Millett (1997). SCITT schemes are also supported and sponsored by Beardon *et al.* (1995) as being the way forward in improving standards in teacher education, with schools in the lead. What they propose, in a 24-point agenda, is the setting up of training schools where 'trainees acquire a battery of skills for successful teaching.' They recognise that teaching is more than a set of skills but do not want to be involved in 'a dangerous indoctrination into a particular set of values' – which presumably is how they see higher education. The 'trendy lefty' rides again! They would like trainees, when they have 'achieved the confidence that goes with the mastery of basic skills' to examine and, if appropriate, reject the values that lie behind them. Alas, they are not at all clear how this can be brought about. Pring (1995) warns against ignoring the complexities of teaching, and of abstracting simple definitions from the wider social and educational traditions. He warns too, of failing to examine the values underpinning subject teaching. This failure, he asserts, will distort what teachers have traditionally been about, 'to introduce the next generation to those ideas and skills and beliefs that have survived critical scrutiny.' He properly raises the question of whether it is possible to become a teacher in a value-free zone.

Quite apart from the argument in principle, the case for SCITT is hardly overwhelming in practice. There are concerns about the quality of provision in SCITT schemes. Anderson (1995) reports involvement in the programme to be 'dependent on one or two enthusiastic individuals' and also reports fairly widespread concern about the lack of preparation time to get a scheme up and running. She does acknowledge benefits, mainly concentrating on students' enhanced understanding about how schools operate and the working life of a teacher. In a list of 'challenges' facing school-centred teacher training, she identifies the need to clarify the role of the mentor, the cruciality of accurate costings which reflect the labour-intensive nature of school-centred schemes and, most importantly, the *sine qua non* of acceptability – the establishment of credible and recognisable criteria of teacher competence and professional development standards. OFSTED (1997), in a report on a Primary SCITT scheme – a substantial consortium – identified a lack of consistency in Quality Assurance procedures, a lack of shared responsibilities and a lack of rigour in monitoring and assessing students, along with serious concerns affecting the quality of provision. By contrast, in similar reports of school and higher education partnerships, during the OFSTED 'primary sweep', primary courses demonstrated that on average, 90 per cent of students were satisfactory or better, with almost half (45 per cent) achieving 'good' or 'very good' levels OFSTED (1995a). These reports confirm 'well established' Quality Assurance arrangements in the Partnerships, OFSTED (1995b). Thus there seems to be a picture emerging in which SCITT schemes are the inferior model. A pertinent question to ask is whether existing partnership schools will continue, in the face of pressures. These include high level inducements to defect to SCITT, OFSTED inspections, constantly changing criteria for assessing students, dwindling resources and innovation fatigue. There is clear evidence that many schools are varying their commitment to partnership from year to year, causing higher education to work with changing partners on a shorter term basis than is desirable.

The role of HE

Although school staffs may be resistant to SCITT, this should not mean that higher education can rest on its laurels. The case for resisting the de-coupling of the profession of teaching from higher education needs to be made. This implies that higher education must state its case. Furlong (1996: 164) urges university staff to work closely with the teaching profession both in the school community and at universities.

> It is, I suggest, equally challenging to bring the culture of HE into school, encouraging teachers to expose their practice to critical scrutiny. The promise of establishing a close and routine dialogue between HE and schools is immense. It is the prize of developing a more genuine discipline of education than we have had in the past – one that is both practical and theoretical.

Several investigations, *Mentoring in Schools* (Campbell and Kane 1996b) being one, suggest differences in the roles of tutors and teachers, especially in the area of the task of promoting in students systematic, critical evaluation of practice in order to refine, renew and develop teaching. That teachers find critical appraisal and evaluation of teaching difficult is not a newly discovered phenomenon. Tutors working in CPD contexts have vast experience of stimulating and encouraging practitioner research amongst teachers. They appreciate the difficulties in supporting teachers to become critically reflective of their own practice. The transfer of this skill to enable students to become so is a challenge, albeit a stimulating one. 'Doing teaching' and 'critically evaluating teaching' are not, of course, mutually exclusive; in fact both are highly desirable. Unfortunately the current problem is that the profession seems to be being pushed into accepting one of these – the 'better lesson' approach – without having the other crucial one. Fish (1995a) urges tutors and teachers to join forces in fighting back against external impositions which work against the development of 'professional artistry' and which reduce HE tutors to mere 'administrators of quality control'. What is becoming apparent is that tutors are more able to take a variety of roles, to move from a very supportive role with students, through to developing wider perspectives on teaching and into a more distant, more objective role encompassing assessment. Questions arise from this conclusion. One would be, whether higher education puts sufficient energy and time into helping teachers develop the ability to evaluate their practice critically, in order to stimulate the same in students? That begs the questions of how this might be done and whether mentors have the capacity to develop these skills. There seems to be abundant evidence that they have such a capacity, but do not always have the time or the know-how.

Higher education emerges from the recent and current national debate, strongly endorsed by Sutherland (1997) as an essential partner. It is generally accepted now that tutors have a great deal of expertise in subject areas, professional studies and in the assessment of students. Mentors, in common with head teachers and many parents and governors, rarely foresee a form of teacher training without a substantial role for higher education. Whilst there is still a long way to go in working out and agreeing who does what and when, in the training of primary teachers, we would not expect to find among teachers substantial support for the move to even more school-based teacher training. This is in tune with the findings of the Modes of Teacher Education Project (MOTE), Whiting *et al.* (1996).

The more schools become involved in partnership, the more the role of higher education attracts favourable comment from school-based partners which is based upon experience and reflection. Selection of schools, moderation, quality control and determining the culture to which students should be exposed would be among those roles. Dangers can be highlighted, 'It is the role of HE to moderate and to be in a consultative role – like calling in the Fire Brigade but it could almost become the Police Force if we are not careful', Campbell and Kane (1996a).

The need for collaborative practice is abundantly clear if partnership is to progress beyond 'a range of different associations. Some of these associations approach genuine partnership. At the other end of the spectrum, some bear more relationship to the 'twinning' of cities: not much more than a notice at the side of the road', Campbell, Hustler and Stronach (1996).

There is a great deal of realism in primary schools, which is why they do not, in general, think they can 'go it alone'. Nor do they think they have the total knowledge or expertise to train teachers alone. Teachers have not the time, the resources nor the access to current literature and evolving practice to educate fully the next generation of teachers. Joint supervision, collaboration and dialogue between teacher–mentors in school, and most crucially between higher education tutors and teachers, is arguably an essential part of school-based training. There is a realisation of the complexity of supervision, the need to be able to select appropriate strategies to suit the context, to enable students to go beyond 'the plateau', to be able to challenge student practice and thinking beyond the obvious classroom management focus. Mentors and tutors alike are centrally concerned with helping students to be able to develop the critical faculties to be able to appraise, evaluate, refine and improve their practice so as to enhance pupil learning; also to be able to share knowledge with other teachers to promote continuing professional development and collective professional understanding and responsibility. Schools and universities are in it together.

FURTHER READING

For an insight into how mentoring affects whole-school development, see Chapter 10 in Edwards, A. and Collison, J. (1996) *Mentoring and Developing Primary Practice: Supporting Student Teacher Learning in School*, Milton Keynes: Open University Press.

For a more general exploration of whole-school approaches, see Bridges, D. (1993) 'School-based teacher education', in Bridges, D. and Kerry, T. (eds) *Developing Teachers Professionally*, London: Routledge.

Michael Fullan's (1993) work on change in education is a useful background; also see Fullan, M. (1991) *The New Meaning of Educational Change*, London: Cassell.

For a report of research into SCITT schemes and Articled and Licensed Teacher schemes, see Anderson, L. (1995) 'Conceptions of Partnership in school-centred initial teacher training', in Bines, H. and Welton, J. (eds) *Managing Partnership in Teacher Training and Development*, London: Routledge.

Various OFSTED documents are available which document the evaluation and inspection of SCITT schemes, *School-Centred Initial Teacher Training* (OFSTED 1995a), and e.g. *17/97/1TTSP Primary Teacher Training* (OFSTED 1997).

For further reading on the contribution of higher education to teacher training, see Chapters 8, 11 and 14 in Furlong, J. and Smith, R. (eds) (1996) *The Role of Higher*

Education in Initial Teacher Training, London: Kogan Page.

For a discussion of values and the curriculum, see Ball, S. J. (1994) *Education Reform: A Critical and Post-Structuralist Approach*, Milton Keynes: Open University Press.

On a similar theme and broadening out the area of discussion see Apple , M. (1996) 'Education, identity and cheap French fries', in Apple, M. *Cultural Politics and Education*, Milton Keynes: Open University Press

PART THREE

CHAPTER 9

Fictionalising the research data

> Much of the impetus behind personal stories is moral. Education is seen correctly as a way to reawaken ethical and aesthetic sensitivities that, increasingly, have been purged from the scientific discourse of too many educators. Or it is seen as a way of giving a voice to the subjectivities of people who have been silenced. There is much to commend in this position. Indeed, any approach that evacuates the aesthetic, the personal and the ethical from our activities as educators is not about education at all. It is about training.
>
> Apple (1996: xiii)

The methodologies underpinning the investigations which form the basis of this book owe much to the voices of the tutors, teachers, students and children who participated in the research. As the introduction claims, it is a different type of book from many other books arising from research projects. The friendly relationships formed during the life of the project and the sometimes personal nature of data collected influenced the decision to 'tell tales'. There is a 'conventional' research report, Campbell and Kane (1996b), and we have drawn extensively from this in the tales. The methodology underpinning The Mentoring in Schools research project was greatly influenced by case study approaches, Macdonald and Walker (1975) and Simons (1980) and by collaborative action research, Elliott (1991). It was rooted also in a practitioner research paradigm common in the Didsbury School of Education's research activity and CPD courses. The research project aimed systematically to investigate mentoring processes and practices in the five primary schools which were in the project, in order to illuminate and evaluate and to provide 'platforms of understanding', Kemmis (1980), for the future development of mentoring and partnership between schools and higher education institutions. Data were gathered via informal interviews with mentors, head teachers and students; journal entries of mentors pursuing their own individual lines of enquiry; schools' team meetings; group discussions; notes and observations from visits to schools. This process of collaborative research, involving mentors and tutors, stimulated a variety of types of writing. These ranged from therapeutic and creative to analytical and ethnographic, as described by Holly (1989). These writings shaped the research project and influenced the way in which the participants viewed it. Through the various individual lines of enquiry undertaken by mentors, insights were gained into a wealth of qualitative data, spanning such issues of a whole-school approach, particularly in Chapter 8, 'Partners: stormy weather'; gender and mentoring as discussed in Sharon's story (Chapter 4); pupils' views of partnership, as documented in Chapter 5, 'Out of the Mouths: child's eye views'; student teachers' views of mentoring in 'De-briefing: triumph and disaster' (Chapter 6); relationships with significant others as discussed in 'The meeting: staff, parents and governors' (Chapter 2); experiences of mentoring as displayed in 'Mentors' stories' (Chapter 7); and students' struggles in the tales of Paula and Mike (Chapters 1 and 3). There can be quality and depth in these insights, as Dadds (1995) acknowledges in her story about Vicki and the action research process, which 'take off the outer layer of perception and there are worlds to discover below'. Similarly, Walker (1981) writes of the attraction of fictional forms that 'they offer a license to go beyond what, as an evaluator/researcher, you can be fairly sure of knowing'.

From such origins came the idea of using stories, or tales.

By presenting the phenomenological aspects of school-based training, and the acutely human side of mentoring, telling how people actually experienced mentoring, we have hoped to rediscover the value of subjectivity and to bring together different strands in education and research. In a similar way Thomas (1995: 4) claimed, 'one unifying aspect (of the qualitative research paradigm) was the affirmation of the actors'/agents' right to speak for themselves: the advent of the teacher as subject not object.'

Putting teachers and their professional and personal concerns centre-stage in the research project, giving them a voice, had a high priority in the subjective approaches adopted by the research team. John Elliott (1995: xii) in his introduction to Dadds' single case study of one teacher, Vicki, comments about objectivity and subjectivity and their reconciliation in small-scale case study research,

> Objectivity is reconciled with a passionate commitment to values, research methods are created to enhance rather than constrain the practical usefulness of research, and the concept of validity is redefined in terms of practical and developmental criteria.

It is hoped, as Dadds says of Vicki, that 'In her story lies the landscape of many untold others'. The tales in this book should have struck chords for the teachers, students and tutors who read them. Through the story of Vicki, Dadds hoped to 'illuminate the contextualised nature of professional development within the shifting ecology of the school culture and within the motivation and power of personal, historical and autobiographical agenda', and to demonstrate the importance and influence of cultural settings on teachers' development. Similarly, we hoped that the tales would provide a rich context for the exploration of mentoring and school-based teacher education.

There has been an increasing volume of writing about school-based teacher education, mentoring and partnership. The issues we have addressed in this book are rarely new. Some of them have been identified in previous research and publications, e.g. McIntyre and Hagger (1993), Jacques (1992), Furlong and Maynard (1995) and Edwards and Collison (1996); but what we hope we have done is to portray, in an account of a single fictional primary school and its inhabitants, issues which are central to the understanding and development of school-based teacher education. There is, hopefully, a coherence achieved by creating a school setting, with characters and situations which will reveal the 'real' researched stories of teachers, pupils and tutors.

Storytelling and narrative discourse are important aspects of everyone's life, helping us to understand and interpret experience. The approach taken in this book, while utilising narrative and story approaches, goes one step further than most biographical studies of teachers' lives and careers by 'creating' tales, and fictionalising the data.

Hardy (1986) called narrative 'a primary act of mind', giving 'storying' a central status in logical thinking and reminded us that the link between 'storying' and theorising is the process of imagination. In a discussion of the uses of fictional critical writing and the use of narrative in research, Winter (1988: 235) acknowledges the difficulty of gaining new insights from research:

> What a researcher wishes to do above all is to generate new insights – insights which only the research has made available – and this is not easy; it is quite hard to avoid merely documenting one's old familiar insights with another layer of data, especially given the limits on the range of data imposed by resourcing constraints.

Winter argues that the contribution of imagination is to introduce 'play' to the process of research and he identifies 'play as the mode of innovative understanding' which allows the researcher to play with 'the actual and potential discontinuities within experience, using metaphorical processes of language to manipulate elements in a state of affairs'.

Thus, the writers of this book have played with the data collected, developing scenarios, creating tales, telling stories, and developing metaphors, while at the same time attempting to formulate and construct arguments for and against theories arising from research into school-based teacher education, mentoring, and partnership ventures.

The identification and analysis of teacher metaphors – especially 'root' metaphors which 'capture a teacher's core self perception', Ball and Goodson (1985) – were used to illuminate teaching practice and to explore an avenue for understanding teaching, by Bullough *et al.* (1991) in their case studies of emerging teachers, which influenced the thinking of the authors as they constructed their tales. It was the intention of the authors, in tune with Winter's (1988) description of a 'montage', to 'undermine the familiar sense of necessary cause and effect and that sense of common-sense unity', by creating fictions which 'surprised' the reader. Winter identifies the works of Brecht, Shakespeare, actual books such as *Catch 22* by Joseph Heller, and 'any episode of *Cagney and Lacey*' as having elements of surprise, and states, 'In other words, a fictional text is not to be taken as imparting knowledge about reality but as raising questions about reality, through the unresolved plurality of its meanings', Winter (1988: 236).

Similarly it was also our intention to involve the reader in a creative examination of the text and to engage in 'the dialectics of reading' and 'to formulate the unformulated', Iser (1974). We also hoped that there might be some fun in it.

Research into narrative and story, undertaken in America, has also been of interest in the compilation of this book. Clark *et al.* (1996), in an article about collaboration in professional development, utilises a 'Readers' Theatre' – a written script – to present story data in a narrative form which aims to incorporate and honour the voices of all participants. Our book seeks, as asserted in Clark *et al.*, to 'challenge traditional conceptions of the roles of teachers and researchers as theorisers about and disseminators of knowledge', by fictionalising the research data and by disguising cases and people. It is hoped that the voices of participants come through as authentic and that there is a realisation of the development resulting from collaborative research among teachers and tutors, 'because of the conversations and dialogues we have shared', Florio-Rouane, (1991). The work of Clandinin and Connelly (1995, 1996) on teachers' professional landscapes has much relevance to the development of the methodological approaches taken in this book, in that their 1996 paper had the belief that 'the professional knowledge context shapes effective teaching' and access to those 'landscapes of knowledge' is best gained through story: 'The professional knowledge landscape inhabited by teachers creates epistemological dilemmas that we understand narratively in terms of secret, sacred and cover stories' (1996: 25).

Stories allow teachers or student teachers to talk 'secretly' among themselves in their 'communities of practice', Lave and Wenger (1991), to talk out of schools and classrooms and tell 'cover stories' which 'fit within the acceptable range of the story of school being lived in the school'. We have included both types of stories in our amalgam of characters and settings. Mike, for example, is both a secret 'real student' story, and also an amalgam of characteristics of other failing students' stories.

Any discussion of the methodology would not be complete without a health warning and a note of caution. Clandinin and Connelly(1996: 28) identify 'the necessary deceptions, as teachers obscure their knowledge by saying one thing and doing another. The telling and living of cover stories may give the impression that teachers do not know what they know. But they do.'

They assert that knowledge from research into effective teaching has caused teachers to devalue their professional knowledge. This is a common feeling amongst teachers in the UK as the effects of inspection, both in school and higher education, impact on the knowledge base for teaching.

The opposite was true of our intentions. We hoped that by telling stories we would give evidence of the complex and integrated nature of teachers' professional knowledge. Apple (1996) warns of too much emphasis on the personal. While acknowledging that the 'personal is political', he worries that the 'political is not always the personal' and that opportunities for reform may be missed if there is too much emphasis on the personal, without due reference to the wider social, cultural and political debates. The commentaries included in this book are an attempt to connect the stories to the wider debates in teacher education, to present a critical commentary and establish a relationship with recent and relevant research in the area of mentoring and school-based teacher education. The book seeks to provide a wider context for the local tales and it attempts to present, in a readable way, the interaction of theory and practice, as experienced by teachers and students in school.

Eisner (1997) enters the debate about addressing the potential strengths and weaknesses of alternative forms of data representation, writing on the theme of 'the cutting edge of inquiry in research methodology'. He relates issues of representation concerning educational research with similar issues in anthropological research. He praises the work of Clifford and Marcus (1986) in 'the crisis of representation' and commends Bruner's (1986) distinction of 'paradigmatic and narrative ways of knowing' as being important and revealing as to the problems being encountered in doing research. Eisner claims that, 'the edges are being explored . . . in the usefulness, in the distinctions between objectivity and subjectivity, the functions of voice in writing, and in the relationship of the general to the particular', Eisner (1997: 6)

He counsels the use of critical reflection and analysis, and the use of a critical community. He sees the need to ask why researchers are interested in alternative forms of representation? Is it because the tools we have are not doing the job as well as they could? He proposes that the search for new forms of data representation is indicative of the growing interest in engendering a 'sense of empathy' for the lives of people. The perils he identifies are a lack of 'referential precision' a lack of recognition of previous research, which locates research in unambiguous fields. He also stresses the need for context, as discussed earlier, as a major requirement for alternative forms which are treading relatively new ground and urges the consideration of the publication constraints related to non-printed forms. He does, however, recognise the 'promise' of the new forms of representation and advises 'exploring the edges'.

Exploring the edge of school-based teacher education through fictional critical writing and tale-telling has, we hope, stimulated interest in further research and investigation, and provided those 'platforms for understanding', Kemmis (1980), as well as opening up the personal, ethical, moral and human side of teacher and student experiences of partnership. The brief snapshot of pupils' views has highlighted the need to consult all participants in school-based partnerships and is one area where the authors hope to continue to research. Readers may also identify and relate to characters, perhaps even recognise in them traits of a well-known tutor, teacher, student, or pupil. Or self.

Epilogue

Most of them lived happily ever after. Derek abandoned his SCITT scheme, but we did spend quite a long time on it at the Staff Development Day. He took a couple of body blows prior to that. His friend Colin raised the matter at the local National Association of Head Teachers (NAHT) meeting and word of Derek's intentions was well and truly out at his cluster meeting shortly after. Neither group saw him as a visionary. In the event his staff were dead against it on the day. Two days before that Wilma got her well-deserved headship, and, as expected, Meg declared that she wanted a two-year moratorium on students for her and her KS1 section. Mark and Tom hung in there enthusiastically, but Derek still needed two more mentors if he was to keep a sizeable stake in teacher training let alone run a SCITT school. He got his new mentors. Damien stepped in from the wings and it seemed that ever since the amazing Mike, Class Next Door had developed an interest in students. Then it transpired that his new Deputy Head, who came from Thames Road school, was keen to take over from Wilma. She had been much involved with our students and with Chris (the Prat). Since then Derek has recruited two NQTs from us. Both are soon to begin their third year and both of them are keen to contribute to the school-based training they felt worked well for them. One of them was David Brown – but only Wilma and I hold the tapes and records of thirty devastating supervision reports. Mark is looking for a deputy headship and I'm confident he'll get one. Tom applied for the Deputy Headship when Wilma left, but, as Derek explained, he was too valuable to bring out of the classroom.

Paula settled down and is teaching successfully in an inner-city school. She's about to enrol on my MEd course. Yvette didn't settle down. She qualified but had more traumas and confrontations and quit altogether during her second year of teaching. Sharon finished with a wonder degree, got a good job, enjoyed her year as an NQT but became very attached to the young man who looked after students and new staff. That wasn't a problem. He'd just split up with his girlfriend who was 'difficult' and not much interested in his job. Meeting Sharon quickly helped him overcome his upset and I have an invitation to their wedding. It's in Southampton. I don't suppose I'll get there but it was a kind thought. Mike is taking Holy Orders. He's at a theological college in Cambridge, where he graduated. He works even more with the local Sunday School classes. That should be worth a call if you're passing St Michael's, Colin's school and Mike's parish. Naturally he contributes massively to the life of the parish when he comes home. He'll be ordained very soon now.

The other students went their various ways. The Two Ronnies struggled through and are 'somewhere in the city'. They could never be 'something'.

Kevin failed, though. He really was a fraud and as the pressure increased, bits began to fall off him. His final practice was a disaster. His repeat was worse. All the others in that group were fine, even Bev. The humiliating experience of that day when her PCS fell apart seemed to make an impression on her as nothing else had done. She passed, satisfactorily, but I'm not sure that if she ends up in a staffroom where lots of the teachers belong to the Opposite Party, then she won't join them. Katie still sends Christmas cards to Tom.

Shortly after Wilma left, OFSTED came to Jemima Johnston. Personally, I think it was a judgement on Derek for his flirting with the SCITT heresy. He needn't have worried. The school did very well. OFSTED said it was extremely well-managed and a keen and enthusiastic staff were 'spiritedly led'. He liked that. They praised his policies and made a special note of the school's contribution to initial teacher training. All of the teachers and their lessons were deemed to be at least satisfactory and the inspectors noted the excellent support given to new and/or inexperienced numbers of staff. Two teachers were 'gazetted'. Unsurprisingly one of them was Meg. I expect you've guessed the other. Yes, it was Tom. He who laughs last . . . That's OFSTED for you.

OFSTED are coming to us again next month to do a special millennium study of primary partnership. I shall be sending them to Jemima Johnston. They always do us proud.

Trish has recently gone back into advisory work. As LEAs began to acquire some previously lost responsibility and as the national drive for literacy gathered momentum, it was clear that her skills and experience were much in demand. She has a big regional coordinator's role now as the Literacy Project moves further into its dissemination and extension phases. She was never really happy with students. She has no children of her own so she hasn't lived through teenage angst and early career crisis. The problem which arose with Mark and Sharon rattled her. Shortly before she left she actually confided in me: 'You don't get that sort of situation with advisory teachers.' I await the rude awakening.

Jeremy is still with us though. He is now deeply into post-modernism. He actually approves of my jottings about Jemima Johnston and the experiences of students and mentors. I told him recently that I was thinking of writing about school-based training but in a fictional format. He thought that was splendid, and quite post-modernist, and there's hope for me yet.

'All fact is fiction,' he said. 'Any account of anything is no more than one person's description of what he or she thinks they are hearing or seeing. For another person it would be totally different. Indeed for the same person it would be similarly different later in the same day. I'll look forward to reading it.'

I don't think I'll write up the stories after all. I couldn't cope with 'similarly different'.

Then again, maybe I will.

Bibliography

Anderson, L. (1995) 'Conceptions of partnership in school-centred initial teacher training', in Bines, H. and Welton, J. (eds) *Managing Partnership in Teacher Training and Development*. London: Routledge.

Apple, M. (1996) 'Education, identity and cheap French fries', in Apple, M. *Cultural Politics and Education*. Milton Keynes: Open University Press.

Ball, S. J. (1994) *Education Reform: A Critical and Post-Structuralist Approach*. Milton Keynes: Open University Press.

Ball, S. and Goodson, I. F. (eds) (1985) *Teachers Lives and Careers*. London: Falmer Press.

Banks, F., Leach, J. and Moon, B. (1996) 'Knowledge, school knowledge and pedagogy: reconceptualising curricula and defining a research agenda'. Paper presented at ECER Conference, September 1996, Seville, Spain.

Beardon, T., Brown, M., Hargeaves, D. and Reiss, M. (1993) 'School-led initial teacher training', in Kerry, T. and Shelton-Mayes, A. (eds) *Issues in Mentoring*. London: Routledge.

Bell, A. (1981) 'Structure, knowledge and relationships in teacher education', *British Journal of Sociology of Education* **2**(1), 3–23.

Bennett, N. and Carre, C. (eds) (1993) *Learning to Teach*. London: Routledge.

Bines, H. and Welton, J. (1995) *Managing Partnership in Teacher Training and Development*. London: Routledge.

Biott, C. and Spindler, J. (1995) 'Learning about primary schools as workplaces: aspects of active staff membership during placements', in McBridle, R. (ed.) *Teacher Education Policy: Some Issues Arising from Research and Practice*. London: Falmer Press.

Bolton, G. (1994) 'Stories at work. Fictional critical writing as a means of professional development. *British Educational Research Journal* **20**, 55–68.

Booth, M. (1993) 'School-based training: the students views', in Booth, M., Furlong, J. and Wilkin, M. (cds) *Partnership in Initial Teacher Training*. London: Cassell.

Boydell, D. (1994) 'Developing a collegial approach to teacher education', *Mentoring: Partnership in Education* **1**(3), 312.

Bridges, D. (1995) 'School-based teacher education', in Bridges, D. and Kerry, T. (eds) *Developing Teachers Professionally*. London: Routledge.

Brown, S. and McIntyre, D. (1993) *Making Sense of Teaching*. Milton Keynes: Open University Press.

Bruner, J. (1986) 'Two modes of thought', in *Actual Minds, Possible Worlds*, 11–13. Cambridge Mass.: Harvard University Press.

Bullough, R. V., Knowles, J. G. and Crow, N. A. (1991) *Emerging as a Teacher*. London: Routledge.

Cameron-Jones, M. and O'Hara, P. (1997) 'Support and challenge in teacher education', *British Educational Research Journal* **23**(1) 15–26.

Campbell, A. and Kane, I. (1996a) 'Mentoring and primary school culture', in McIntyre, D. and Hagger, H. (eds) *Mentors in School: Developing the Profession of Teaching*. London: David Fulton Publishers.

Campbell, A. and Kane, I. (1996b) Research Report *Mentoring in Schools*. The Manchester Metropolitan University: Didsbury School of Education.

Campbell, A., Hustler, D., and Stronach, I. (1996) 'Partnership: how many partners can one partnership have without getting a bad reputation?' Paper given at British Educational Research Association (BERA) Conference, September 1996, Lancaster University.

Campbell, A., Cockett, P., Peckett, J. and Whiteley, M. (1998 in press) 'Across the Great Divide: what can be learned from an investigation of primary and secondary partnerships?' in Hudson, A. S. and Lambert, D. (eds) *Exploring Futures in Teacher Education: Changing Key for Changing Times*. London: Institute of Education.

Carney, S. and Hagger, H. (1996) 'Working with beginning teachers: the impact on schools', in McIntyre, D. and Hagger, H. (eds) *Mentors in Schools: Developing the Profession of Teaching*. London: David Fulton Publishers.

Clandinin, D. J. and Connelly, F. M. (1995) *Teachers' Professional Knowledge Landscapes*. New York: Teachers' College Press.

Clandinin, D. J. and Connelly, F. M. (1996) 'Teachers; Professional knowledge landscapes: teacher stories – Stories of teachers – School stories – Stories of schools', *Educational Researcher* **25**(3) 24–30.

Clarke, C., Moss, P., Goering, S., Herter, R. J., Lamar, B., Leonard, D., Robbins, S., Russell, M., Templiss, M. and Wascha, K. (1996) 'Collaboration as dialogue: teachers and researchers engaged in conversation and professional development', *American Educational Research Journal*, Spring 1996, **33**(1) 193–231.

Claxton, G. (1989) *Being a Teacher: A Positive Approach to Change and Stress*. London: Cassell.

Clifford, J. and Marcus, G. (eds) (1986) *Writing Culture: The Poetics and Politics of Ethnography*. Berkeley, Calif.: University of California Press.

Craig, B., and Kane, I. (1994) *Similarities and Differences: Interim Report No.1* Mentoring in Schools Project, Didsbury School of Education, The Manchester Metropolitan University.

Crowther, G. (1995) 'A primary school view of involvement in initial teacher training', in Bines, H. and Welton, J. (eds) *Managing Partnership in Teacher Training and Development*. London: Routledge.

Dadds, M. (1995) *Passionate Enquiry and School Development: A Story About Teacher Action Research*. London: Falmer Press.

Daloz, L. (1986) *Effective Teaching and Mentoring*. San Francisco: Jossey Bass.

Day, C. (1993) 'Reflection: a necessary but not sufficient condition for professional development', *British Educational Research Journal* **19**(1), 83–93.

DES (1991) *School-based Initial Teacher Training in England and Wales*. London: HMSO. (The 'Brown Book')

Devlin, L. (1995) 'The mentor', in Glover, D. and Mardle, G. (eds) *The Management of Mentoring: Policy Issues*. London: Kogan Page.

DfEE (1997) *Teaching, High Status, High Standards* – Circular 10/97.

Downes, P. (1996) 'The changing balance in initial teacher education: a school perspective', in Furlong, J. and Smith, R. (eds) *The Role of Higher Education in Initial Teacher Education*. London: Kogan Page.

Doyle, W. (1986) 'Classroom organisation and management', in Wittrock, M. C. (ed.)

Handbook of Research on Teaching. New York, Macmillan.

Dreyfus, H. L. and Dreyfus, S. E. (1986) *Mind Over Machine: The Power of Human Intuition and Expertise in the Era of Computers*. New York: Macmillan

Dunne, E. and Bennett, N. (1997) 'Mentoring processes in school-based training', *British Educational Research Journal* **23**(2), 225–37.

Dunne, R. and Harvard, G. (1993) 'A model of teaching and its implications for mentoring', in McIntyre, D., Hagger, H. and Wilkins, M. (eds) *Mentoring: Perspectives on School-based Teacher Education*. London: Kogan Page.

Edwards, A. (1997) 'Guests bearing gifts: the position of student teachers in primary school classrooms', *British Educational Research Journal* **23**(1) 27–37.

Edwards, A. and Collison, J. (1996) *Mentoring and Developing Practice in Primary Schools: Supporting Student Teacher Learning in School*. Milton Keynes: Open University Press.

Edwards, A. and Knight, P. (1994) *Effective Early Years Education*. Milton Keynes: Open University Press.

Edwards, T. (1995) 'The politics of partnership', in Bines, H. and Welton, J. (eds) *Managing Partnership in Teacher Education and Development*. London: Routledge.

Egan, G. (1990) *The Skilled Helper: A Systematic Approach to Effective Helping*, 4th edn. Pacific Grove, Calif.: Brooks/Cole.

Eisner, E. W. (1997) 'The promise and the perils of alternative forms of data representation', *Educational Researcher* **26**(6), September.

Elliott, B. and Calderhead, J. (1993) 'Mentoring for teacher development: possibilities and caveats', in McIntyre, D., Hagger, H. and Wilkin, M. (eds) *Mentoring: Perspectives on School-based Teacher Education*. London: Kogan Page.

Elliott, J. (1991) *Action Research for Educational Change*. Milton Keynes: Open University Press.

Elliott, J. (1995) 'Introduction', in Dadds, M. *Passionate Enquiry and School Development: A Story About Teacher Action Research*. London: Falmer Press.

Feiman-Nemser, S. and Buchmann, M. (1987) 'When is student teaching teacher education?', *Teaching and Teacher Education* **3**, 255–73.

Feiman-Nemser, S. and Rosaen, C. (1997) (eds) *Guiding Teacher Learning: Insider Studies of Classroom Work with Prospective and Practising Teachers*. Washington: American Association of Colleges for Teacher Education.

Ferguson, P. and Womack, S. T. (1993) 'The impact of subject matter and education course work on teaching performance', *Journal of Teacher Education* **44**, 66–72.

Firth, T. (1993) Episode 3 of *All Quiet on the Preston Front*. BBC.

Fish, D. (1995a) *Quality Mentoring for Student Teachers: A Practical Approach to Practice*. London: David Fulton Publishers.

Fish, D. (1995b) *Quality Learning for Student Teachers: University Tutors' Educational Practices*. London: David Fulton Publishers.

Florio-Rouane, S. (1991) 'Conversation and narrative in collaborative research: an ethnography of the written literacy forum', in Witherell, C. and Noddings, N. (eds) *Stories Lives Tell: Narrative and Dialogue in Education*, 234–56. New York: Teachers' College Press.

Fullan, M. (1991) *The New Meaning of Educational Change*. London: Cassell.

Fullan, M. (1993) *Change Forces: Probing the Depths of Educational Reform*. London: Falmer Press.

Fullan, M. and Hargreaves, A. (1992) *What's Worth Fighting For in Your School?* Milton Keynes: Open University Press.

Furlong, J. (1992) 'Reconstructing professionalism: ideological struggle in initial teacher education', in Arnot, M. and Barton, L. (eds) *Voicing Concerns: Sociological Perspectives on Contemporary Education Reforms*. Wallingford: Triangle Books.

Furlong, J. (1995) 'The limits of competence: a cautionary note', in Kerry, T. and Shelton-Mayes, A. (eds) *Issues in Mentoring*. London: Routledge.

Furlong, J. (1996) 'Do students need Higher Education?' in Furlong, J. and Smith, R. (eds) *The Role of Higher Education in Initial Teacher Education*. London: Kogan Page.

Furlong, J. and Kane, I. (1996) *Recognising Quality in Initial Teacher Education*. Occasional Paper No. 6, University Council for the Education and Training of Teachers.

Furlong, J. and Maynard, T. (1993) 'Learning to teach and models of mentoring', in McIntyre, D., Hagger, H. and Wilkin, M. (eds) *Mentoring: Perspectives on School-based Teacher Education*. London: Kogan Page.

Furlong, J. and Maynard, T. (1995) *Mentoring Student Teachers: the Growth of Professional Knowledge*. London: Routledge.

Furlong, J. and Smith, R. (eds) (1996) *The Role of Higher Education in Initial Teacher Training*. London: Kogan Page.

Furlong, J., Whitty, G., Whiting, C., Miles, S., Barton, L. and Barrett, E. (1996) 'Redefining partnership: revolution or reform in initial teacher education?', *Journal of Education for Teaching* **22**(1), 39–55.

Glenny, G. and Hickling, E. (1995) 'A developmental model of partnership between primary schools and higher education', in Bines, H. and Welton, J. (eds) *Managing Partnership in Teacher Training and Development*. London: Routledge.

Graham, J. (1997) 'Transformative partnership; towards a strategy for collaborative professional action'. Paper given at Standing Conference for Education and Training of Teachers (SCETT) Conference, Autumn 1997, Dunchurch, Rugby.

Hardy, B. (1986) 'Towards a poetics of fiction', in *Novel: A Forum*. Providence, RI: Brown University.

Harlen, W. (1996) 'Primary teachers' understanding in science and its impact in the classroom'. Paper presented at British Educational research Association (BERA) Conference, September 1996, Lancaster University.

Heil, R. and Jones, C. (1997) (eds) *New Teachers in an Urban Comprehensive School: Learning in Partnership*. Stoke-on-Trent: Trentham.

Hogbin, J., Cockett, P. and Hustler, D. (1996) 'Diversity, change and continuity: developing institutional policy at the Manchester Metropolitan University', in Hustler, D. and McIntyre, D. (eds) *Developing Competent Teachers: Approaches to Professional Competence in Teacher Education*. London: David Fulton Publishers.

Holding, D. H. (Ed) (1989) *Human Skills*, 2nd edn. Chichester: Wiley.

Holly, M. L. (1989) *Writing to Grow*. Portsmouth, NH: Heinemann.

Hoyle, E. (1982) 'Micropolitics of educational organisations', *Educational Management and Administration* **10**, 87–98.

Hustler, D. and McIntyre, D. (eds) (1996) *Developing Competent Teachers: Approaches to Professional Competence in Teacher Education*. London: David Fulton Publishers.

Iser, W. (1974) 'The reading process: a phenomenological approach', in Cohen, R. (ed.) *New Directions in Literacy History*. London: Routledge and Kegan Paul.

Jacques, K. (1992) 'Mentoring in initial teacher education', *Cambridge Journal of Education* **22**(3), 337–50.

John, P. D. (1996) 'The subject method seminar and the role of the teacher educator', in Furlong, J. and Smith, R. (eds) *The Role of Higher Education in Initial Teacher Training*. London: Kogan Page.

Kelly, M., Beck, T. and ApThomas, J. (1992) 'Mentoring as a staff development activity', in Wilkin, M. (ed.) *Mentoring in Schools*. London: Kogan Page.

Kemmis, S. (1980) 'The imagination of the case and the invention of the study', in Simons, H. *Towards a Science of the Singular*. CARE Occasional publication No. 10, Norwich, University of East Anglia.

Lave, J. and Wenger, E. (1981) *Situated Learning: Legitimate Peripheral Participation*. Cambridge: Cambridge University Press.

MacBeath, J. (1994) 'A role for parents, students and teacher in school self evaluation and development planning', in Riley, K. A. and Nuttall, D. L. (eds) *Measuring Quality: Education Indicators – UK and International Perspectives*. London: Falmer Press.

Macdonald, B. and Walker, R. (1975) 'Case study and the philosophy of educational research', *Cambridge Journal of Education* **5**(1), 2–11.

Mardle, G. (1995) 'The consequences', in Glover, D. and Mardle, G. (eds) *The Management of Mentoring*. London: Kogan Page.

Maynard, T. (1996) 'Mentoring subject knowledge in the primary school', in McIntyre, D. and Hagger, H. (eds) *Mentors in Schools: Developing the Profession of Teaching*. London: David Fulton Publishers.

Maynard, T. (ed.) (1997) *An Introduction to Primary Mentoring*. London: Cassell.

McCulloch, M. and Locke, N. (1994) 'Mentorship developments in the primary phase of initial teacher education at the University of Reading', *Mentoring and Tutoring* **1**(3), 21–28.

McIntyre, D. (1992) 'Theory, theorising and reflection in initial teacher education', in Calderhead, J. (ed.) *Conceptualising Reflection in Teacher Development*. London: Falmer Press.

McIntyre, D. and Hagger, H. (1993) 'Teachers' expertise and models of mentoring', in McIntyre, D., Hagger, H. and Wilkin, M. (eds) *Mentoring: Perspectives on School-based Teacher Education*. London: Kogan Page

McIntyre, D. and Hagger, H. (eds) (1996) *Mentors in Schools: Developing the Profession of Teaching*. London: David Fulton Publishers.

McIntyre, D., Hagger, H. and Wilkin, M. (eds) (1993) *Mentoring: Perspectives on School-based Teacher Education*. London: Kogan Page.

Meredith, A. (1995) 'Terry's learning: some limitations of Shulman's Pedagogical Content Knowledge', *Cambridge Journal of Education* **25**(2), 176–87

Millett, A. (1997) Letter to schools, 14 May 1997. London: TTA.

Moon, B. and Shelton-Mayes, A. (1995) 'Integrating values into the assessment of teachers in initial education and training', in Kerry, T. and Shelton-Mayes, A. (eds) *Issues in Mentoring*. London: Routledge.

Moyles, J. (1995) 'The road to Damascus: learning from continuing experiences', in Moyles, J. (ed.) *Beginning Teaching: Beginning Learning, in Primary Education*. Milton Keynes: Open University Press.

OFSTED (1993) *Curriculum Organisation and Classroom Practice in Primary Schools: A*

Follow Up Survey. London: OFSTED.

OFSTED (1995a) *School-centred Initial Teacher Training 1993–94*. Report from the Office of Her Majesty's Chief Inspector of Schools. London: HMSO.

OFSTED (1995b) *Partnership: Schools and Higher Education in Partnership in Initial Teacher Training*. Report from the Office of Her Majesty's Chief Inspector of Schools. London: HMSO.

OFSTED (1997) *Report 17/97/ITTSP, Primary Teacher Training*. London: OFSTED. ('The Primary Sweep')

OFSTED/TTA (1996) *Framework for the Assessment of Quality and Standards*. London: OFSTED/TTA.

Pacific Institute (1997) *Investing in Excellence: Materials and Programme*. Seattle: Pacific Institute.

Pring, R. (1993) 'Standards and quality in education', in Kerry, T. and Shelton-Mayes, A. (eds) *Issues in Mentoring*. London: Routledge.

Reich, M. (1995) 'The mentor connection', in Kerry, T. and Shelton-Mayes, A. (eds) *Issues in Mentoring*. London: Routledge.

Rhodes, G. (1994) 'Managing the beginning teacher in school', in Wilkin, M. and Sankey, D. (eds) *Collaboration and Transition in Initial Teacher Training*. London: Kogan Page.

Richardson, R. (1990) *Daring to be a Teacher*. Stoke-on-Trent: Trentham Books.

Rowlands, S. (1990) 'The power of silence: an enquiry through fictional writing', *British Educational Research Journal* **17**(2), 95–111.

Schunk, D. H. and Meece, J. L. (1992) *Student Perceptions in the Classroom*. Hillsdale, NJ: Lawrence Erlbaum Associates.

Senge, P. (1992) *The Fifth Discipline: The Art and Practice of the Learning Organisation*. London: Century Business.

Shaw, R. (1992) 'Can mentoring raise achievement in school?', in Wilkin, M. (ed.) *Mentoring in Schools*. London: Kogan Page.

Shaw, R. (1993) *Teacher Training in Secondary Schools*. London: Kogan Page.

Shulman, L. (1986) 'Those who understand knowledge growth in teaching', *Educational Researcher* **15**, 4–14.

Simons, H. (ed) (1980) *Towards a Science of the Singular*. CARE Occasional publication, No. 10. Norwich: University of East Anglia.

Sparkes, A. C. and Mackay, R. (1996) 'Teaching practice and the micropolitics of self preservation', *Pedagogy in Practice* **2**(i), 3–22.

Stephens, P. (1997) 'Student teachers' concerns and accomplishments on main school placements: what school mentors can learn from them', *Mentoring and Tutoring* **5**(1).

Stoll, L. and Fink, D. (1996) *Changing Our Schools*. Milton Keynes: Open University Press.

Suschitzky, W. and Garner, B. (1995) 'It takes two to tango! Working with experienced others in the school', in Moyles, J. (ed.) *Beginning Teaching: Beginning Learning in the Primary School*. Milton Keynes: Open University Press.

Sutherland, S. (1997) Report No. 10 'Teacher education and training: a study', National Committee of Inquiry into Higher Education: The Dearing Enquiry, London: HMSO.

Thomas, D. (1995) 'Treasonable or trustworthy text: reflections on teacher narrative studies', in Thomas, P. (ed.) *Teachers' Stories*. Milton Keynes: Open University Press.

Thomas, D. (ed.) (1995) *Teachers' Stories*. Milton Keynes: Open University Press.

Thompson, M. (1997) *Professional Ethics and the Teacher: Towards a General Teaching Council*. Stoke-on-Trent: Trentham Books.

Tickle, L. (1993) 'The wish of Odysseus? New teachers' receptiveness to mentoring', in McIntyre, D., Hagger, H. and Wilkin, M. (eds) *Mentoring: Perspectives on School-based Teacher Education*. London: Kogan Page.

Tomlinson, P. (1995) *Understanding Mentoring*. Milton Keynes: Open University Press.

TTA (1995) *Teachers Make a Difference: A Research Perspective on Teaching and Learning in Primary Schools*. London: TTA.

Turner, M. (1995) 'The role of mentors and teacher tutors in school-based teacher education and induction', in Kerry, T. and Shelton-Mayes, A. (eds) *Issues in Mentoring*. London: Routledge.

Walker, R. (1981) 'On the uses of fiction in educational research', in Smetherham, D. (ed.) *Practising Evaluation*. Driffield: Nafferton.

Watkins, C. and Whalley, C. (1995) 'Mentoring beginner teachers – issues for schools to anticipate and manage', in Kerry, T. and Shelton-Mayes, A. (eds) *Issues in Mentoring*. London: Routledge.

Weber, M. (1948) *From Max Weber: Essays in Sociology*, H. H. Gerth and C. Wright Mills (trans and ed.). London: Routledge, Kegan and Paul.

Welton, J., Howson, J. and Bines, H. (1995) 'Managing partnership: future directions', in Bines, H. and Welton, J. (eds) *Managing Partnership in Teacher Training and Development*. London: Routledge.

Whiting, C., Whitty, G., Furlong, J., Miles, S. and Barton, L. (1996) *Partnership in Initial Teacher Education: A Topography*. MOTE Project, Institute of Education, London.

Whitty, G. (1995) 'Quality control in teacher education', in Kerry, T. and Shelton-Mayes, A. (eds) *Issues in Mentoring*. London: Routledge.

Whitty, G. and Willmott, E. (1995) 'Competence-based teacher education: approaches and issues', in Kerry, T. and Shelton-Mayes, A. (eds) *Issues in Mentoring*. London: Routledge.

Wilkin, M. (1990) 'The development of partnerships in the United Kingdom', in Booth, M., Furlong, J. and Wilkin, M. (eds) *Partnership in Initial Teacher Training*. London: Cassell.

Winter, R. (1988) 'Fictional critical writing: an approach to case study research by practitioners and for inservice and pre-service work with teachers', in Nias, J. and Groundwater-Smith, S. (eds) *The Enquiring Teacher*. London: Falmer Press.

Woodhead, C. (1997) Letter to selected schools, 23 May 1997. London: OFSTED.

Woods, P. (1995) *Creative Teachers in Primary Schools*. Milton Keynes: Open University Press.

Woods, P. and Jeffrey, B. (1996) *Teachable Moments: The Art of Teaching in Primary Schools*. Milton Keynes: Open University Press.

Index